LEARNING SOCIAL OR ORGNIZATIONAL CULTURE

HOW INFLUENCE ECONOMY

JOHN LOK

Contents

Preface

Introduction

This book research any countries culture improvement can assist themselves economic growth. I shall follow three aspects to research this question. The first aspect researchs whether the country researchs talent human experiment which can help any businessmen to raise productivities or efficiencies. The second aspect researchs whether the country encourages employers apply high technological environment, it can raise productivities or efficiencies, the final researchs whether the country encourages over time working environmental culture, whether it can raise productivities or efficiencies.

The first research aspect concerns how talent human can be created successful. What are the differences between talent human and common human IQ? How to evaluate the person has special talented human and excellent abilities? What aspects do we need to train talent human to attribute our society? Which kinds of talent human shortage to our society nowadays?

Our future will need different kinds of talent human to attribute their abilities to let our society to develop in success. So, future talent skillful training is very important . If our future society can train talent human in success, then our society will have more chance to achieve any unpossible missions, e.g. Mar living exploration, undiscovered natural resource exploration, artificial intelligent technological development, new medical medicine invention etc. different missions, which is waiting our talent humans attribute their unique knowledge to achieve these any one of missions in success. Hence, talent human training is essential. How can we train talent human in success. We must know what methods will have possible to achieve training any kinds of talent human in success.

This first research will indicate some methods to explain how to achieve training talent human plan in success. It is suitable to any readers have interest to know what methods can train talent human in possible success.

This second research explains any countries culture improvement can assist themselves economic growth, in special high technological productive environmental culture. I shall follow three aspects to research this question. The first aspect researchs whether the country researchs talent human experiment which can help any businessmen to raise productivities or efficiencies. The second aspect researchs whether the country encourages employers apply high technological environment, it can raise productivities or efficiencies, the final researchs whether the country encourages over time working environmental culture, whether it can raise productivities or efficiencies.

The final research concerns whether labors abnormal long time working hours working culture which can influence society economic growth and raises productivity in long time. Why do I choose to research this topic? Because I discovered many employers need labors to increase working hours to work often, such as China , Hong Kong etc. developing countries. Although, they feel this method will help them to reduce to spend salary or wage expenditure to employ extra full time labors to assist them to achieve to raise aim of productivity. But in fact, they neglect to consider other disadvantages to cause their labors to feel tiring and unfair treatment and reduce their stanrdard of life, due to their labors will not increase salary or wage very much and who also need to work very long hours per working day. Hence, I shall indicate evidences to prove why abnormal work hours method can only raise productivity in the short term, but this method can not raise productivity in the long term and it can also influence overall society economic decline and it can also influence labors' standard of life to be poor. In the final, I shall also recommend how employers, such as Hong Kong and China employers how to change their methods to achieve to raise their productivity in the long term. This book is suitable to any readers have interest to research how culture impovement can bring any countries' economic growth in possible.

Prologue

CHAPTER I

Training Super Talent Human Culture

When one country encourages any businessmen provide different kinds of trainings to let their employees to learn, whether these learning training organizational cultures can help employees to raise working efficiencies or improve performance. In behavioral economic view, whether training culture can help the country's overall economy raises productivies and improve performance, even raises economic growth or brings economic benefits to any firms. Want a Superior Workforce? How to Develop a High-Performance Workforce ? A superior workforce is one that is collectively better than an average workforce. It often includes employees who are smarter, faster, more creative, harder working, insightful, aware of the competition, and autonomous. They are daily contributors to a harmonious workplace that emphasizes accountability, reliability, and contribution.

If your goal is a superior, high-performance workforce that is focused on continuous improvement, you need to manage people within a framework that focuses on performance management and development.To achieve this, there are seven components you need to implement. They work together to create a superior, high-performance workforce. Create a checklist to implement these components and to make sure you are following through regularly.

1. Hiring

Create a documented, systematic hiring process. Ensure that you hire the best possible staff for your superior workforce:

· Define the outcomes desired from the people you hire.

· Develop job descriptions that clearly outline the performance responsibilities.

· Develop the largest pool of qualified candidates possible. Search via professional associations, social media networking sites such as LinkedIn, online job boards, personal contacts, employee referrals, university career services offices, search firms, job fairs, newspaper classifieds, and other creative sources when necessary.

· Devise a careful candidate selection process that includes culture match, testing, behavioral interview questions, customer interviews, and tours of the work area.

· Perform appropriate background checks that include employment references, employment history, education, criminal records, credit history, drug testing, and more.

· Make an employment offer that confirms your position as an employer of choice.

2. Defining Goals

Provide the direction and management needed to align the interests of your high-performance workforce with your organization's goals and desired outcomes:

· Provide effective supervisors who give clear direction and expectations, provide frequent feedback, and demonstrate the commitment to staff success.

· Company direction, goals, values, and vision should be communicated frequently and in memorable ways when possible.

· Provide a motivating work environment that helps employees want to come to work every day.

· Provide an empowering, demanding, commitment-oriented work environment with frequent mention of company goals to support your high-performance workforce.

3. Reviewing Progress

Hold quarterly performance development planning (PDPs) meetings to establish aligned direction, measurements, and goals:

· Performance and productivity goals and measurements that support your organization's goals should be developed and written.

· Personal development goals should be agreed upon with individual employees and written. These can range from attendance at a class to cross-training or a new job assignment.

· Most importantly, progress on the performance development goals is tracked for accomplishment. Central tracking by Human Resources ensures the development of the entire workforce.

4. Feedback

Provide regular feedback to employees that lets them know where they stand:

· Effective supervisory feedback means that people know how they are doing daily, via a posted measurement system, verbal or written feedback, and meetings.

· Develop a disciplinary system to help people improve areas in which they are not performing as expected. The system is written, progressive, provides measurements and timelines, and is regularly reviewed with staff members.

5. Employee Recognition

Provide a recognition system that rewards and recognizes people for real contributions:

· Provide equitable pay with a bias toward variable pay using such methods as bonuses and incentives. Whenever possible, pay above market.

· Develop a bonus system that recognizes accomplishments and contributions.

· Design ways to say "thank you" and other employee recognition processes such as company periodic anniversary remembrances, spot awards, team recognition lunches, and more. You are limited only by your imagination.

· Despite the rising cost of health care insurance, which you may need to share with your employees, provide a continually improving benefits package.

6. Training

Provide training, education, and development to build a superior, high-performance workforce:

.Employee retention and education begins with a positive employee orientation. Employee orientation should give new hires a complete understanding of the flow of the business, the nature of the work, employee benefits, and the fit of his or her job within the organization.

· Provide ongoing technical, developmental, managerial, safety, lean manufacturing, and/or workplace organization training and development regularly. The type of training depends on the job. Some experts recommend 40 or more hours of training a year per person.

· Develop a procedure-based, cross-training matrix for each position that includes employee skill testing and periodic, scheduled, on-the-job training and demonstration of capability, for most hands-on jobs.

· Provide regular management and leadership training and coaching from both internal and external sources. The impact of your frontline people on the development of your high-performance workforce is critical.

· Create jobs that enable a staff person to do all the components of a whole task, rather than pieces or parts of a process.

· Develop a learning organization culture through such activities as "lunch and learn," reading books as a team (book club), attending training together, and by making the concept of continuous learning an organization goal.

· Make a commitment to both providing and tracking the accomplishment of the developmental activities promised in the PDPs.

7. Employment Termination

End the employment relationship if the staff person is not working out:

· If you have done your job well—effective orientation, training, clear expectations, coaching, feedback, support—and your new staff person is failing to perform, termination of employment should be swift.

· View every termination as an opportunity for your organization to analyze its hiring, training, integrating, support, and coaching practices and policies. Can you improve any aspect of your process so the next new employee succeeds?

· Perform exit interviews with valued employees who leave. Debrief the same as you would a termination situation.

· Use an employment ending checklist to make certain you have wrapped up all loose ends.

Training method can be applied to employees. Similarity, training method can be also applied to super-athlete sport man.How to Grow a Super-Athlete ? I believe that training must need to grow a super-Athlete. I shall indicate how and why training is needed to grow a tennis super athlete sportman.

The future of tennis training?
A quick analysis of this talent map reveals some splashy numbers: for instance, the average woman in South Korea is more than six times as likely to be a professional golfer as an American woman. But the interesting question is, what underlying dynamic makes these people so spectacularly unaverage in the first place? What force is causing those from certain far-off places to become, competitively speaking, superior?

So even here, at the core of one of the globe's brightest talent blooms, the question of that talent's source remains enigmatically tangled, perhaps as much of a mystery to those who nurture these athletes as it is to the rest of us. It's enough to make you wish for a set of X-ray glasses that could reveal how these invisible forces of culture, history, genes, practice, coaching and belief work together to form that elemental material we call talent — to wish that science could come up with a way to see talent as a substance as tangible as muscle and bone, and whose inner workings we could someday attempt to understand.

However, basketball or tennis sport men, talent is not one main factor cause their super skill raising. Training is one important factor causes their super skill raising. "This is a new dimension that may help us understand a great deal about how the brain works, especially about how we gain skills."

Its very inertness is why the first brain researchers named their new science after the neuron instead of its insulation. They were correct to do so: neurons can indeed explain almost every class of mental phenomenon—memory, emotion, muscle control, sensory perception and so on. But there's one question neurons can't explain: why does it take so long to learn complex skills?

"Everything neurons do, they do pretty quickly; it happens with the flick of a switch," Fields said. "But flicking switches is not how we learn a lot of things. Getting good at piano or chess or baseball takes a lot of time, and that's what myelin is good at."

To the surprise of many neurologists, it turns out this electrical tape is quietly interacting with the neurons. Through a mechanism that Fields and his research team described in a 2006 paper in the journal Neuron, the little sausages of myelin get thicker when the nerve is repeatedly stimulated. The thicker the myelin gets, the better it insulates and the faster and more accurately the signals travel. As Fields puts it, "The signals have to travel at the right speed, arrive at the right time, and myelination is the brain's way of controlling that speed."

"What do good athletes do when they train?" George Bartzokis, a professor of neurology at U.C.L.A., had told me. "They send precise impulses along wires that give the signal to myelinate that wire. They end up, after all the training, with a super-duper wire — lots of bandwidth, high-speed T-1 line. That's what makes them different from the rest of us."

It also left me thinking about the clusters on the talent map. Specifically, wondering whether these places quietly possess myelin-accelerating factors: i.e., forces and conditions that promote what Fields would call "circuit optimization." Might those factors help explain the success of these superior athletes?
Hence, I feel that training is one important factor to manufacture super sport man and super employee. Talent is not the important factor to manufacture super sport man and super employee.

● The talent management skill
raises organizational development
and motivation of employees
When human primitive society is farming primary industry, farmers are only using hand to grow any kinds of plants, vegetable, fruit , rice to sell. Then, the farming work system was organized in primary forms using simple tools and with the least expertise and with division of duties in farm tasks. But in developed farming society, the farming work division is complicated, the farming duties are specialized, and the use of advanced farming technology, such as one farming vehicle can replace farmers' hand to grow any kinds of plants on farms.

The science of growing technology can help any plants to grow in fast speed and kill any animals, they can hurt plants to grow easily. This is good example of human talent technique development in farming industry. It can increase any kinds of plants growing of efficiency in fast speed and short time growing in order to raise plants, fruit food productivies.

If human talent technique can be applied to our business society. Can human talent technique help any organization job characteristics raising efficiency and intrinsic motivation is more for the employees that are satisfied with their growth, and the employees with more experience were more satisfied with supervisor and collegues.

How can organizations apply talent management technique to raise work quality of the employees and their attempts? If any organizations hope to raise employee motivation. They need to concern how to change any job forms of content, job process to be more attractive. In order to achieve employees motivation more efficiently. For example, if the organization's employees can be motivated by more payments, fewer work hours, and suitable work condition. This kind of organizational talent management method ought bring employees motivation can be increased through providing independence and responsibility of the employees. The question concerns: Which factor or which factors motivate each employee in any organizations? Because every organization has different characteristics and different job title and duty. Some every organization factors motivate employees, they ought be different. Every organization ought focus on why individuals choose certain behavioral alternatives for satisfaction of needs in order to seek what factor(s) can increase its employees' motivation. Hence, if the organization has high degree of job motivation and satisfaction. The organization can predict the organizational commitment positively. So, it seems that one high degree of job motivation an satisfactory organization can bring high employee productivities turnover.

Organizational strategic talent method aims to create an accessible source of talents for adapting the right individuals with the right jobs and the right time based on the strategic purposes of business. Because the lack of talent is the biggest obstacle on the lack is a kind of major strategic advantage. Hence, any organization managers must need to know how to manage talents. How to use the individuals and how strategically to place them in proper position. Managers must design the situation to have the maximum knowledge and information, innovation and effort. And identify and discover whom are talents scarce and underdeveloped resources, how to seek talented employees. Such as talent labor market, it has key factors influence the efficiency of entering the labor market. These factors are the analysis of the current labor market situation and the rational preference of specialization. The active search and the talent employees interviewing, talent employees labor market search, these components are any organizations' talent recruitment essential method, if they hope to recurit any talented people to serve their organizations absolutely. Instead of talent recruitment factor, the other factors influence organizational success. They may include: Whether the organization has implemented feedback surveys, sensitivity training, management network, practical research, and training the techniques of improvement of intrapersonal relationships. So, those soft skills will be any successful organizations' essential talent management methods. So, organizations can not neglect any one of these factors in order to employee talented people to serve their organizations effectively.

● What is strategic talent management skill?
Strategic talent management skill can maximize the competitive advantage of an organization's human capital, this talent management is even more significant to be needed in nowadays organizational management, e.g. how to develop a talent pool of high potential and high performance to fill the organizatons' any roles as well as how to develop in differentiated human resource strategy to facilitate filling these positions with competent and to ensure all employees are talent to continue commitment to the

organizations.

It is important to note that key positions are not necessarily restricted to the top management team (TMT), but also include key positions at levels lower than the TME and many vary between operating units and time. The reason is because any organization ought not need a stable top position, and this top position ought may be variable any time.

For one bank organization example, it ought not only CEO top position. It ought follow its market need to change CEO position, e.g. sometimes the bank may have more than one CEO position, e.g. share selling division CEO, housing loan division CEO, investment division CEO. Moreover, the lower position , such as manager can also increase to two or more, e.g. house loan division can have one CEO manager two housing loan department managers, even more. If the house loan division needs to increase staffs number to do any loan administration, loan applicaion and loan confirmation tasks in the house loan clients number busy time. So, bank top management CEO and lower management manager positions number can not ought keep only one. It is one wrong talent management strategy. It ought follow the client number to decide how to increase the right employees number in order to decide whether the bank's any department ought employ one CEO or manager position or more in order to solve the bank clients need number. Because if the bank only have one CEO and manager to manage their department. They will feel difficulty, if employees and bank clients number are increasing suddenly. They will feel busy and feel stressful. So, the bank ought need to decide whether the only one CEO and one manager to every department in busy time. It is suitable to its any departments to cooperate efficiently. Because if its any one department's management is inefficient, then it will influence employee performance and client dissatisfaction. So, the bank talent management method is that any time changes CEO and manager number to any department. Hence, organizational talent management depends on employees, clients number , market need, labor market supply factors.

● Talent culture in the world of work benefits

Talent in the world of work concerns talent management , high performers, high potentials and talent workforce segmentation. Talent should refer to a person's recurring patterns of thought, feeling or behavior that can be productivity applied. The sum of a person's abilities, his or her intrinsic gifts, skills, knowledge, experience, intelligence, judgement, attitudes, character and drive. Talent can be considered as a complex employees' skills, knowledge, cognitive ability and potential. Employees' values and work preferences are also of major importance, a select group of employees, those that rank at the top in terms of capability and preference, rather than the job, times commitment, willing to do the job, times contribution finding meaning and purpose in their work.

Hence, a talent person or worker who ensures the competitiveness, and future of a company as specialist or leader, through his organizational job specific qualification and knowledge , his social and methodical competencies, ans his characteristic attributes , such as eager to learn or achievement oriented. A talent person or worker has these characteristics: competence, knowledge, skills and values required for today' and tomorrow's job, right skills, right place, right job, right time and contribution , finding meaning and any nowadays talent person's characteristics.

Does talent refers to people (subject) or to the characteristics of people (object) ? Is talent more about performance, potential , competence, or commitment? Is talent a natural ability or does it relates more to further improving through practice? Talent is typically associated with athletes (e.g. Olympians, exceptional coaches, extraordinary teams, musicians of extraordinary ability, singers with incredible voices). It is commonly understood as above-average ability for a specific function or range or functions. Rather than corresponding to " normal" ability, talent is considered a special ability that makes the people who posses, develop and use it in the specific area of their talent.

Consequently, talent is often meant to excellent performance in a given performance domain. But in working society, talent has another meaning, i.e. people posses special skills or abilities. For job advertisement in which talent refers to potential applicants (e.g. talent wanted).

Talent is as a kind of natural ability, more than training to own personal skills capacity. In general, talent person owns a unique mix of innate intelligence or brain power, and a certain degree of creativity or the capacity to go beyond estabished stereotypes and provide innovative solutions to problems in his everyday life more easily to compare common people.

In general, common people or student or worker can be taught to own skills and knowledge to learn easily. But , talent has characteristics much more unique. Therefore, talent is impossible to learn or teach easily. It is the person innate nature owns, talent can not really managed by any persons or organizations easily, because talent is always a function of experience and effort, e.g. an excellent sport person can be trained to be one excellent sport skillful talent person, even he has not one talent sport skillful person to any kinds of sport, e.g. riding bicycle, sport. If the sport person is not excellent in riding bicycle sport, but if he has a good trainer, he can teach good riding bicycle method or skill to be trained him to be one riding bicycle sporter. Then, for a long time riding bicycle learning perios, he will have possible to be one talent riding bicycle sport person. So, in some situaton, one non-talent learner will be trained to be one talent learner, if the trainer has good skills and methods to teach the trainee, such as riding bicycle sport case, it is not all riding bicycle sport person is one talent sport man. Their excellent riding bicycle skills need to be trained to raise their riding bicycle skills. Then, their talent on riding bicycle skills will be raised to be performed in possible. So, for sport man case, talent is not natural, talent sport man (trainee) is trained by trainer. Hence, creating a talent person, it depends on these factors: The right place, the right position, and/or the right time. Such as the riding bicycle sport trainee case, he needs have right riding bicycle learning school , e.g. riding bicycle facility, good quality bicycle and large bicycle indoor spor place to let the bicycle sport trainee to learn. Then, he also needs a good trainee to learn. Then, he also needs a good bicycle teaching trainer , he can teach good riding bicycle skill and fast speed riding and safe riding knowledge to let him to ride his bicycle in the riding bicycle competitive games in the fastest speed safely in order to win his riding bicycle competitors.

Finally, right time is also important factor, if in the time, the riding bicycle trainee has physical body hurt challenge or poor emotion psychological challenge. These factors will influnce his riding bicycle learning performance or abilities in order to achieve the best performance level. So, he needs to wait the time, he has good physical health and good emotion psychological time, then he can learn his riding bicycle trainer's riding bicycle knowledge and skill easily. Hence, one talent sport man needs have above these thress basic requirements: right place, right position, right ime in order to achieve the talent sport man training in success.

● Building high performance culture talent management method to organizations

Any human decision making can influence our organizations value. How our culture causes may influence how we can fall serve to our organization? Our organization culture can influence how we bring energy, creativity and enthusiasm to our organization value. So, it brings these questions concern how our organizational culture can bring high performance to our organization productivity , such as:

How can our talent management to our organization culture can bring consequence on increasing profits and shareholder value, attracting and keeping talented people, building brand loyalty, ensure that ethic corporate culture to achieve high performance. Also, how out talent management to our organization culture can help we deliver high quality , cost effective services and a sustainable society service. The key questions concern how building a high performance culture to our private and public sector organizations. We need to know that the culture of an private organization's source comes from its competitive advantage and brand differentiation, as well as the culture of an public organization source comes from its cost effectiveness and quality of services.

Hence one successful public and private organization cultures may bring these performance effects: values and behaviors drive cutlure, culture drives employee fulfilment, employee fulfilment drives customer satisfaction and mission achievement. Because any organizational staff's cultural behavior, their principles, ideas, or briefs that people (staffs) can influence organizational operation. For example, similarly, if the organization has potentially limiting value of bureaucracy, that it can cause rigidity and limit the free idea expression from any staffs. This organization cultural value will limit employees' personal value and poor financial peformance because it's organizational cultural value is not " open mind" or let employees have chance to share their opinions to discuss their company any issues very easily.

So, bureaucracy cultural value will be weakness to any organizations, e.g. some countries' government organization is bureaucracy cultural value. It can not innovate or raise or improve its government internal organization different departments' efficiencies very easily. But, it needs lone time to do any decisions . It is a bureaucracy organization's weakness or easy cooperation between the values of the culture of the organization and the personal values of employees, the final effect is low performance, which can further resultin low levels of staff engagement and poor quality of products and services. All these bureacucracy organization's long time decision making and messages need long time delivery factors can have a significant impact on the financial performance or low efficiency (inefficiency) of the organization or its ability to deliver services of low quality.

Hence, if the organization's culture is able to attract and retain talented individuals. This gives organizations a significant commercial advantage, especially when talent is in short supply.

Strong brand values are always those with the strongest internal cultures. So, it has relationship between high cultures, brand differentiation, or retaining talented individuals and the successful is highly dependent on the culture that the leaders create.

Also, the culture that leaders create is highly dependent on the behaviors of the leaders and their relationship to other leaders in the organization, and their relationships with their employees. It explains that why organizations with strong , high performing cultures tend to replace their leaders by promoting from within, whereas low -performing cultures tend to replace their leader's with external candidates. The reason is because that by promoting from within, organization's good cultures are also to retain their successful leadership styles. However, organization's culture and desired leadership styles is one kind of management feeling from all employees and managers working behavior and attitude. Any organizations must need spend time to research what their organization culture is and what leaders desired leadership styles are.

How can we know our organization culture is suitable to let our low level and high level employees accept to work together? We can follow those change to judge whether our organization's culture is suitable organization culture. The change may include: A different way of doing. Doing what we do now, but doing it in a more efficient, productive, or quality -enhancing way, a different way of being. Transformation involves changes at the deepest levels of beliefs, values and assumptions. Transformation occurs when we are also be learnt from our mistakes, are open to a new future, and can let revise of the part mistakes.

Hence talent retention is critically important for all organizations for two main reasons: Turnover is expensive and top performers drive business performance. Turnover costs arise from the direct replacement costs of talent acquisition, the opportunity costs of vacant positions and time to productivity, in the result costing of business performance. Hence, one organization has good cultural value, it may have characteristics: The organization can have confidence to recruit the right people in the first place, it can improve the line manager's ability to manage, it can give employee's constrant feedback about clear, meaningful goals, it can empower employees to manage their own careers, it can continuously measure and improve retention strategies easily. All of these are any good cultural organization's characteristics.

Hence, talent managemen may a key aspect of human resources management strategy in any organizations? In this age of the rapily expanding knowledge-based economy, the quality of human resources has assumed crucial importance. This complex and demanding market environment has a demand for outstanding and talented with high development potential, being the lever of growth in shareholder value. The organization talent leader has attitude, a performance -oriented approach, the ability to persuade, teamwork, emotional intelligence, flexibility, a high tolerance to change, and highly developed specialist technical skills. However, it has relationship between developing talent people and good organizational culture. Because developing talent people and good culture, then it can develop talent people easily.

How can we know that the organization has good culture. Similarly, if we discover that the organization has many talent people are working, then we may assume that the organization has good organizational culture . We can follow how many employees' talent level, they own and they are working in the organization. The talent level can consist of these several points: Extraordinary intellectual skills (general and specialist), a creative attitude (originality, flexible thinking and acting, solving unconventional problems easily, and a high tolerance to risk, change , uncertainty) and a commitment to work (self-disciplined, persistent in pursuing goals, and hard-working). Hence, if the organization has many employees, who own extraordinary intellectual skills, a creative attitude, a commitment to work attitude. Then, I believe that the organization owns many talent suitable to let them to feel to work.

Hence, what is talent management cultural organization? A talent management cultural organization can ensure that talent people are attracted, retained, motivated and developed in line with the needs of the organization, i.e. the most valuable staff memebers, by creating conditions conducive to their potential development. So that they can be put to use for the company's operations for as long as possible, talent management is a set of activities taken vis-a vis personnel with outstanding talents to ensure their development and increase their operational efficiency, when immediately achieve corporate goals easily. A talent management cultural organization consists of searching for talents inside or outside the organization, undertaking special activities to enable their development, training and career path planning and ensuring that their remuneration is competitive with that of other organizations, talent management involves implementing a set of key activities as part od human resource management , when immediately applying more advanced methods and techniques.

Hence, one talent management cultural organization ought own above all these characteristics. A talent management cultural organization can reduce employee turnover number, they can keep talent people continue stay to work in their organization for long time. So, when the organization's workforce (employee leaving) turnove rate reduces, in special talent employees, then its high performers and employees with hard-to-replace skills, these group employees will continue work in their present employers for long time.

Similarly, any talent management cultural organization really can prove itself is one successful organization , it must need long time to learn or improve itself strategy in order to attract many talent employees choose itself organization to work. Hence," learning how to attract talent employee method", which is a important factor to influence whether the organization can be one talent management cultural organization in success.

How can a digital platform one online talent platform assist organizations to recruit talent people? Online talent platforms can ease a number of these dysfunctions by more effective connecting individuals with work opportunities. Labor markets are arriving in the form of digital platforms, the very same technologies that have reshaped the businesses and consumer environment in areas , such as e-commerce.

Online talent platforms are marketplaces and tools that can connect individuals to the right work opportunities. The size of their user networks expand the pool of possibilities, and their powerful search capabilities in an efficient and personalized way. These digital platforms are rapidly popular, acceptable to apply on online talent recruitment method for any organizations.

Talent online recuritment platforms can help companies transform or change the traditional recruitment way or method. They hire, train and manage their employees. All this online talent recruitment method can give better-informed decisions about human capital produce better business results. In additions, online talent recruitment platform could improve signaling about the skill that are actually in demand across the economy. As this information shapes decisions about education and training, the entire skills mix of the economy could adjust more accurately over time.

Online talent recruitment platforms can take form of websites mobile apps, or proprietary corporate systems. They gather a huge volume of information regarding both individual workers and employers or work projects, then synthesize this data to match individuals with job opportunities and produce better work outcomes.

One online talent recruitment platform is a digital tools that enable users (organizations) to post full time or part time jobs, create online resumes of individuals, search for talent or work opportunities, based on extended matching attributes, provide personal working experience and qualification data into company or worker reputations, skills, assess candidates' attributes, skills or fit, personalize onboarding, training and talent management optimize team formation and internal matching, determine the best options for training and skill development.

Hence, online recruitment talent management platform will be a good tool to any organizations' human resource department talent employee choice method to help them to select the most talent employee(s) to work in the right position and in right time. It can replace the traditional newspapers applicant recruitment method or outsoucing job agent applicant recuriment method or government labor department post recruitment method. When one organization has many employees, e.g. 100, even 1000, 10000 or more employees number. Online talent recruitment platform can help it to reduce to spend much time to choose whom are the right applicatns to apply the job position, because (artificial intelligence) AI technology can replace human's judgement ability, it's judgement accurate level may exceed to human judgement level to choose the right applicants to enter the next interview stage. So, it explains that why online talent recruitment platform can replace any organization's human resource department's CV sceening process. It is one good (AI) online recruitment platform to help any recruiters' CV sceening process to be avoided, when (AI) online recruitment CV screening platform method is invented to assist any large organizations' human resource department to reduce time and staff nervous to do every applicant's CV screening activity. This is one good talent management application and recruitment and selection method to any large organizations' large human resource recruitment process.

● Can non-training cultural organizations create talent employees to raise efficiencies

Any organizations must have young age employees to work. If they lack enough training to improve every young employees performance in long time non-training cultural environment. Do these organizations can keep long term talent development to raise employees efficiencies or improve performance. Among young people are potential philosophers, artists, writers, entrepreneurs, whether training method is one important factor to create or manufacture any one of young peole to be super talent person successfully in our society. Some psychologists or behavioral scientists or doctors believe that formal educational (school) training is only the important method to train super talent young people. But, other some psychologists or behavioral scientists or doctors , they argue that formal educaiton (school) training is not the main method to create any one super talent young person in our society.Otherwise, they also feel that non-formal educaiotn method will be easily to create or manufacture one real super talent person in our society nowadays.

I agree the later professional groups' view point any more. I believe that the young person himself/herself free learning
atitude factor is the most influential method to attract any one capacity within the young person to be one super talent person in society in possible more. The super talent young people can discover or seek whether what the real capability, they own in success. They have these same characteristics: They can spend time to attempt to seek whether what their talent capability may own in order
to develop their talent capabilities. Moreover, they do not need any teachers to teach how they may discover their talent capabilities in success in classrooms. Otherwise, they accept to spend their extra non-schooling time to seek whether what kind of talent capabilities , they may own in habit. Because when they feel what kind of talent capabilities that they may own in possible, then they will have habitual behaviors to be creative and innovative to their specialized talent undiscovered capabiliities often. Due to their accumulative time creates
and innovates and concentrate on learning their one kind of talent capability, then they can enhance their the ability of non-formal education learning experience method to create or upgrade or raise the kind of their talent capabilities easily.

The question concerns: How do these common young people not need training method to create or innovate or raise
their talent capabilities to become one super talent young person in success? In fact, any one super talent person, he/she

must be common person in past long time before. It depends on whe he/she can discover or seek whether what the real talent capability that he/she may own in order to upgrade or raise himself/herself this kind of talent capability in success. Even, when he/she knows or ensures that

this kind of talent capability , he/she has owned really. He/she also needs long time to learn in order to upgrade or raise this kind of talent capability. SO, any one super talent young person must need long time to learn the kind of capability in order to be the kind of capability super talent young person.

Hence, it explains why school formal educaiton can not train any super talent students focus on one kind of capability in success. Schools can only provide one group students classroom learning environment to train any one common lazy student to be hard student to attempt to earn high grade to each subject in order to graduate to seek any kinds of occupation in achievement in our society. Otherwise, any one super talent owning one kind of capability at least person, who will not need school learning training method.

They need to spend time to discover any one kind of talent capability , that they own in possible in order to attempt to learn how to upgrade or raise their this kind of themselve owning capability to be raised to super talent capability level, e.g. some super talent pinano music tool player, when he/she feels interest to play pinano music tool, then he/she will spend extra time to learn how to play this kind of pinano music

tool in order to create many good pinano music to let audiences to listen. They do not feel formal education training method can raise their playing pinano music tool skill. They choose to learn from themselves at home in their extra time. So, non formal education learning method has more successful chance to train one common pinano music player to be one super talent pinano music player to compare formal education learning method consequently.

Hence, young people need know how to create and innovate their capacities by themselves. This positive attitude is important in enhancing young peoples' innovative and creative potential in ways that are relevant to employability. It seems that non-formal learning method can support innovation and creativity in young people to their undiscovered capabilities to be upgraded or raised. Any countries government need to spend time to invest non-formal education method to raise young people to discover and learn what their talent capabilities are. The non-formal eduational talent young capabilities plan aims and strategies and outputs may include as below:

It's goals is investment in non-formal learning , leadning to increased capacity for innovation and creativity in young people in ways relevant to employability,
enhancing user-freindly and efficient procedures and methods for recognition of non-formal learning in the development of innovation and creativity skills.

Targets set with indicators to provide signs of progress achievement. The implementing strategies can support non-formal education workers, especially youth workers, who work directly with young people, to raise the quality of provision, such as improving the recognition and validation of non-formal learning, providing (AI) artificial intelligent , robust and accessible tools and resources to support the talent young people capabilities discovering work. Developing partnership working relationship between business and the formal education and non-formal sector, closing the gap between requirements of the labour market and the contribution of no-formal school learning, enhancing entreprensurial skills in young people.

In conclusion, non-formal school or non-formal training learning method or student himself/herself learning method can bring outputs to manufacture or create super talent young peron more easily to compare formal school learning method, e.g. one school teach 100 students, it won't create any one super talent capability of student easily. Otherwise, 100 young people who can spend extra time to learn how to upgrade or raise themselves owning capabilities at home. Any of one or more than one these

100 young people will have more chance to learn to become one super talent person who owns this kind of capability by himself/herself in success when he/she can accept to spend long time to learn by himself/herself. The reaon is that teachers can not persuade they discover to learn themselves capabilities more easier from themselves. So, one non-formal learning method can achieve these outputs, such as improved procedures and better use of non-formal learning method to measure and accredit non-formal learning, better use of methods to measure and access formal learning , improved provision of training and support for non-formal education workers, effective partnership between labour market and education (formal and non-formal) sectors, promotion of non-formal learning through financial support , technical advice, networks and databases, experiments to develop specific areas of practice. However, instead of young people need to spend time to discover what themselves interests or capabilities are and learn them, the another most importance to achieve non-formal education method successful factor is that the expert group will assist itself country

government to work with formal and non-formal partners to ensure that ideas from social scientific research, literature, practice wisdom, policy and discovering any kind of capability consultation processes, inform understandings of any individual young person problems, situations and issues, as well as ideas about

work that can enable desired outcomes and ways of monitoring and evaluating any individual young person himself/herself " capability discovery work" in order to create talent young person mission in success.

CHAPTER II

Technological improvement culture raises economic growth

● Technological cultural improvement
consumer behaviors
High technological improvment cultural globalization refers to the transmission of ideas, meanings, and values around the world in such a way as to extend and intensify social relations. This process is marked by the common consumption of cultures that have been diffused by the Internet, popular culture media, and international travel.

This has added to processes of commodity exchange and colonization which have a longer history of carrying cultural meaning around the globe. The circulation of cultures enables individuals to partake in extended social relations that cross national and regional borders. The creation and expansion of such social relations
is not merely observed on a material level. Cultural globalization involves the formation of shared norms and knowledge with which people associate their individual and collective cultural identities. It brings increasing interconnectedness among different populations and cultures. Hence, I believe that any countries' cultures must have direct factor to infuence consumption market in nowadays socities.

Economic problem – sometimes called the basic or central economic problem – asserts that an economy's finite resources are insufficient to satisfy all human wants and needs. Economics involves the study of how to allocate resources in conditions of scarcity However, viewing economics as the study of how society allocates resources can lead to conflation of normative economic planning and empirical study of how economic agents operate in these conditions.

In mainstream neoclassical economics, it is assumed that humans pursue their self-interest, and that the market mechanism best satisfies the various wants different individuals might have. These wants are often divided into individual wants (which depend on the individual's preferences and purchasing power parity) and collective wants (which are the wants of entire groups of people). Things such as food and clothing can be classified as either wants or needs, depending on what type and how often a good is requested. However, economists have sometimes characterized "how" to produce as a "technological problem" of efficiency whereas the allocation of what is produced is an "economic problem". In a free market, the "how" of production and allocation of resources is distributed among economic agents. In a centrally planned economy, a principal decides how and what to produce on behalf of agents. Modern economies are often welfare capitalist with various regulations, which makes the economic system more equitable while retaining the distributed free market system. Due to human wants are unlimited, an infinite series of human wants remains continue with human life. Nobody can claim that all of his wants have been satisfied and he has no need to satisfy any further want. Everybody feels hunger at a time then other he needs water. Sometime one feels the desire of clothing then starts to feel the desire of having good conveyance. When all existing wants are satisfied then new wants starts to create in mind, so the series of wants remains continue till the last moment of life. So an economic problem arises because of existence of unlimited human wants.

● Problem of allocation of resources to high technological cultural organizations

The problem of allocation of resources arises due to the scarcity of resources, and refers to the question of which wants should be satisfied and which should be left unsatisfied. In other words, what to produce and how much to produce. More production of a good implies more resources required for the production of that good, and resources are scarce. These two facts together mean that, if a society decides to increase production of some good, it has to withdraw some resources from the production of other goods. In other words, more production of a desired commodity can be made possible only by reducing the quantity of resources used in the production of other goods.

The problem of allocation deals with the question of whether to produce capital goods or consumer goods. If the community decides to produce capital goods, resources must be withdrawn from the production of consumer goods. In the long run, however, [investment] in capital goods augments the production of consumer goods. Thus, both capital and consumer goods are important. The problem is determining the optimal production ratio between the two.

In fact, in our societies, resources are scarce and it is important to use them as efficiently as possible. Thus, it is essential to know if the production and distribution of national product made by an economy is maximally efficient. The production becomes efficient only if the productive resources are utilized in such a way that any reallocation does not produce more of one good without reducing the output of any other good. In other words, efficient distribution means that redistributing goods cannot make anyone better off without making someone else worse off. (See Pareto efficiency.) So, scientists will apply efficient distribution methods to help any countries to earn the absolute advantages when we buy and sell any kinds of products or food between ourselves countries, e.g. when US has good natural resource to grow any food, e.g. potato, wheat , vegetable, cotton , then US can export to sell to China, because China has no any farms to grow agriculture food to supply itself Chinese to eat. So, China must need to buy any agriculture food from US. Otherwise, China has cheap labor to supply to US any manufacturers to help them to manufacture their electronic products. SO, it has many US factories are built in China to let Chinese workers help them to produce their products because their wages are cheaper to compare US workers. So, comparative economic advantage will be choice to apply between US and China both countries. (Absolute advantage trade theory)

The inefficiencies of production and distribution exist in all types of economies. The welfare of the people can be increased if these inefficiencies are ruled out. Some cost must be incurred to remove these inefficiencies. If the cost of removing these inefficiencies of production and distribution is more than the gain, then it is not worthwhile to remove them.

● The problem of full employment of resources to high technological cultural organizations

In view of how to use available resources are fully utilized is an important one. A community should achieve maximum satisfaction by using the scarce resources in the best possible manner—not wasting resources or using them inefficiently. There are two types of employment of resources:

(1) Labour-intensive

(2) Capital-intensive

In capitalist economies, however, available resources are not fully used. In times of depression, many people want to work but can't find employment. It supposes that the scarce resources are not fully utilized in a capitalistic economy.

● The problem of lacking high technological cultural organizations whether it can keep economic growth to the country

If productive capacity grows, an economy can produce progressively more goods, which raises the standard of living. The increase in productive capacity of an economy is called economic growth. There are various factors affecting economic growth. The problems of economic growth have been discussed by numerous growth models, including the Harrod-Domar model, the neoclassical growth models of Solow and Swan, and the Cambridge growth models of Kaldor and Joan Robinson. This part of the economic problem is studied in the economies of development.

● Needs and wants problems to the country lacks high technological organizational cultures

Needs are things or material items of peoples need for survival, such as food, clothing, housing, and water. Everyone has a different needs and wants. Until the Industrial Revolution, the vast majority of the world's population struggled for access to basic human needs. Wants are effective desires for a particular product, or for something that can only be obtained by working for it. While the fundamental needs of survival are key in the function of the economy, wants are the driving force that stimulates demand for goods and services. To curb the economic problem, economists must classify the nature and different wants of consumers, as well as prioritize wants and organize production to satisfy as many wants as possible.

● Five bases problems of lacking high technological cultural countries

In our societies , in general, our societies will have these similar problems The following points highlight the five basic problems of an economy. The problems are: 1. What to Produce and in What Quantities? 2. How to Produce these Goods? 3. For whom is the Goods Produced? 4. How Efficiently are the Resources being utilized? 5. Is the Economy Growing?.

Problem 1:What to Produce and in What Quantities?
The first central problem of an economy is to decide what goods and services are to be produced and in what quantities. This involves allocation of scarce resources in relation to the composition of total output in the economy. Since resources are scarce, the society has to decide about the goods to be produced: wheat, cloth, roads, television, power, buildings, and so on. Once the nature of goods to be produced is decided, then their quantities are to be decided. How many tones of wheat, how many televisions, how many million of power, how many buildings, etc. Since the resources of the economy are scarce, the problem of the nature of goods and their quantities has to be decided on the basis of

priorities or preferences of the society.

If the society gives priority to the production of more consumer goods now, it will have less in the future. A higher priority on capital goods implies less consumer goods now and more in the future. But since resources are scarce, if some goods are produced in larger quantities, some other goods will have to be produced in smaller quantities. Suppose the economy produces capital goods and consumer goods. In deciding the total output of the economy, the society has to choose that combination of capital goods and consumer goods which is in keeping with its resources.

Problem 2: How to Produce these Goods?

The next basic problem of an economy is to decide about the techniques or methods to be used in order to produce the required goods. This problem is primarily dependent upon the availability of resources within the economy. If land is available in abundance, it may have extensive cultivation. If land is scarce, intensive methods of cultivation may be used. If labour is in abundance, it may use labour- intensive techniques; while in the case of labour shortage, capital-intensive techniques may be used.

The technique to be used also depends upon the type and quantity of goods to be produced. For producing capital goods and large outputs, complicated and expensive machines and techniques are required. On the other hand, simple consumer goods and small outputs require small and less expensive machines and comparatively simple techniques.

Further, it has to be decided what goods and services are to be produced in the public sector and what goods and services in the private sector. But in choosing between different methods of production, those methods should be adopted which bring about an efficient allocation of resources and increase the overall productivity in the economy.

Problem 3. For whom is the Goods Produced?

The third basic problem to be decided is the allocation of goods among the members of the society. The allocation of basic consumer goods or necessities and luxuries comforts and among the household takes place on the basis of among the distribution of national income. Whosoever possesses the means to buy the goods may have then. A rich person may have a large share of the luxuries goods, and a poor person may have more quantities of the basic consumer goods he needs.

Problem 4: How Efficiently are the Resources being Utilised?

This is one of the important basic problems of an economy because having made the three earlier decisions, the society has to see whether the resources it owns are being utilized fully or not. In case the resources of the economy are lying idle, it has to find out ways and means to utilize them fully.

Problem 5: Is the Economy Growing?

The last and the most important problem is to find out whether the economy is growing through time or is it stagnant. If the economy is stagnant at any point inside the production possibility curve, it has to be moved on to the production possibility curve PP whereby the economy now produces larger quantities of consumer goods and capital goods. Economic growth takes place through a higher rate of capital formation which consists of replacing existing capital goods with new and more productive ones by adopting more efficient production techniques or through innovations.

All of these economy problems will be our societies often causes to anyone feels need to solve problems in order to achieve our societies can have enough resources to satisfy our every day living.

● The Consumer Problem in one lacking high technological manufacturing cultural countries

Consumer theory is concerned with how a rational consumer would make consumption decisions. What makes this problem worthy of separate study, apart from the general problem of choice theory, is its particular structure that allows us to derive economically meaningful results. The structure arises because the consumer's choice sets are assumed to be defined by certain prices and the consumer's income or wealth. The consumer's problem is to choose that is most preferred or, equivalently, that has the greatest utility.

The assumption of perfect information is built deeply into the formulation of this choice problem, just as it is in the underlying choice theory. Some alternative models treat the consumer as rational but uncertain about the products, for example how a particular food will taste or a how well a cleaning product will perform. Some goods may be experience goods which the consumer can best learn about by trying ("experiencing") the good. In that case, the consumer might want to buy some now and decide later whether to buy more. That situation would need a different formulation. Similarly, if the agent thinks that high price goods are more likely to perform in a satisfactory way, that, too, would suggest quite a different formulation. Agents are price-takers. The agent takes prices p as known, fixed and exogenous. This assumption excludes things like searching for better prices or bargaining for a discount.

Hence , it seems that economic problems and consumer problems are similar, I feel that it is possible , economists can attempt to apply any economic theories to solve some consumer problems in some situations. They can find the accurate solutions when they can apply the suitable economic theories to solve the suitable consumer or economic problems in our societies. I shall indicate that how economists can apply the suitable economic theories to attempt to solve some consumer problems in our societies as below:

Demand And Supply Theory Solves Consumer Problems in one owning technological cultural country

What is economy rule predict consumer behaviour? Why and How does economist can apply economy rule to predict consumer behaviours? I shall explain the reasons as below:

Why does economic principle be the best to predict consumer behaviour. It may include these two reasons: The first focuses on the substantive domain of study, in this interpretation , economics is a social science devoted to understanding how the economy works. The second definition focuses on methods: economics is a way of doing social science, using particular tools. In this interpretation the discipline is associated with formal modelling and statistical analysis rather than particular hypotheses or theories about the economy. Therefore, economic methods can be applied to many other areas besides the economy, everything from decisions within the family to questions about political institutions. I believe that one high technological cultural country can apply high technological tool to help them to solve any consumer problems more easily as below:

● Demand and supply principle predict public transport tool passenger behaviour

Economists need to use the right economic ideas to predict consumer behaviour. So, Misuse the wrong economy ideas to predict consumer behaviours. It will do more wrong judgement to evaluate or predict why and how and when the country's consumer behaviours will change. It is every economist needs to consider issue. For example, the economy idea application of economic supply-demand principles to public transport. Different fares would give commuters with more-flexible hours the incentive to avoid peak travel times. They would allow passenger traffic to spread out over time, reducing the pressure on the public transport system when enabling even larger total passenger flow. IT aims to reduce traffic congestion, increased public-transport use, reduced car-bon emissions and cause air pollution and generated considerable revenue for the country's transport system. So, if the country can apply supply and demand economic principle to attempt to predict how many passengers number needs to catch transport tools to go to work or go to school or other activities. Then, it can predict how many bus, ferry, taxi, train, underground train, tram etc. different public transport tools to satisfy future public transport passengers' needs in society. So, this demand and supply principle is the comparative best rule to predict any kinds of public transport passengers' road needs, when they need to either go to school, go to office, go to leisure or shopping etc. different kinds of activities. So, applying the demand and supply principle to predict road and sea public transport passengers can help the country to reduce air pollution when they feel that they can find any public transport tools to catch any time conveniently , then it can encourage them to reduce car purchase desire. When many people choose to catch public transport tools, then it will reduce many cars number on the road. Then, air pollution will reduce as well as any public transport tools' income will also increase as well as traffic jam will also reduce. When the country can evaluate how many people choose to catch bus or taxi or ferry or train or underground train, or tram or train etc. different kinds of public transport tools, then the country can predict the more accurate public transport tools number to every kind of public transport tool to satisfy their journey needs. e.g. whether underground train or train or tram need to decrease or increase the frequent times or number to catch the volume of passenger in busy or non-busy time; or whether bus company has need to increase how much buses to catch the city location passengers when they are living in the city. Moreover, supply and demand principle can help any public transport tools to explain why their passengers number reduces in the year, it may due to fare charge is unreasonable, feeling uncomfortable to sit on the seat or air condition is poor in the transport tool environment, or there are no more seats because many there are much time is full passenger and no seat vacancy to provide to them to sit . So, supply and demand principle can help any kinds of public transport tools to find whether which is (are) the factor(S) can influence the current or last year passengers number reduce. Then, they can concentrate on improving their weaknesses to raise their service quality . So, supply and demand principle can also help they to evaluate whether what their weakness are in order to improve to increase passengers number. They can do questionnaires to enquiry their passengers' response to evaluate whether which areas of services that they feel unsatisfactory. So, the different kinds of service satisfactory feeling to the passengers number data will be the main source to help the kind of public transport tool to analyse and conclude the results more accurate, then they can make the more accurate judgement to improve the of service. For example, the questionnaires indicate that the many passengers feel the bus fare is reasonable, but many passengers feel they can not find any seats to sit easily. So, it implies that the bus firm ought buy more buses or enlarges bus size and increases more seats in the enlarged buses. Then, it does not reduce its fare but it needs to find solutions to let passengers can find seats to sit in every bus more easily. But, if the questionnaires indicate that there are many passengers feel its fare is higher or unreasonable to compare other kinds of public transportation tools. Hence, it can avoid to spend more expenditure to increase bus number to the city, if the city has many passengers , they still choose bus to catch, but they feel its fare is too higher to compare other kinds of public transport tool. Then, it only needs to reduce its fare , it ought help it to increase passengers number. Hence, demand and supply principle is the most suitable economic method to evaluate any kinds of public transport system passenger needs in any country nowadays.

● Supply and demand and price elasticities principle predict oil energy user behaviour

The another case is that demand and supply principle can predict oil buyer behaviour to find whether what factors can cause the oil buyer individual need reduces. For example , a rise in production costs increases market prices and reduces quantities demanded and supplied. Or when, energy cost rise, utility bills increases and households fid extra ways of saving heating and electricity. But, others are nor. For example, whether a tax is imposed on the producers or consumer of a commodity, say oil has nothing to do with who ends up paying for it. The tax might be administered on oil companies, but it might be consumers who really pay for it through higher prices at the pump. Or the extra cost might be imposed on consumers in the form of a sale tax, but the oil companies might be forces to absorb it through lower prices. It all depends on the " price elasticities" of demand and supply. With the addition of extra assumption, this model also generates rather strong implications about how well markets work. In particular, a competitive market economy is efficient in the sense that it is impossible to improve one person's well-being without reducing somebody.

● Demand and supply principle can misuse to predict consumer behaviour when the two firms participate advertisement to promote their products in the same time

Why can demand and supply principle misuse to predict consumer behaviour when the two firms participate advertisement to promote their products in the same time ? I shall explain as below: Assume that two competing firms must decide whether to have a big advertising budget. Advertising would allow one firm to steal some of the other's customers. But when they both advertise, the effects on customer demand cancel out. The firms end up having spent money needlessly.

We might expect that neither firm would choose to spend much on advertising, but the model shows that this logic is off base. When the firms make their choices independently and they care only about their own profits, each one has an incentive to advertise, regardless of what the other firm does. When the other firm does not advertise, you can steal customers from it if you do advertise, when the other firm does advertise, you have to advertise to prevent loss of customers. So, these two firms end up in a bad equilibrium in which both have to waste resources. This market can not apply demand and supply principle to predict consumer behaviours because they depends advertisement to promote their products. If these two firms advertise their products in the same time. Then , it is not possible that if one firm increases it price and it will cause its customer number loss, due to its advertise can help it to attract customers to consider its product from television or radio or newspapers or magazine promotion channels. So, I suppose that these two firms decide to increase their price, when they advertise their products to let customers to know in the same time. They will not lose their customers or reduce their customers easily. Because their customers can be persuaded to choose to buy their products to compare other similar products in preference. So, their increasing price will not influence their customers number lose easily. It explains that demand and supply principle is not right to this case, so demand and supply principle can misuse to help them to predict consumer behaviours when they advertise their products in the same time. Also, demand and supply principle is not suitable to them to predict consumer behaviours when they advertise their products in the same time. They will do wrong prediction to their consumers purchase desire when they advertise their products in the same time.

ON conclusion, using these demand and supply and price elasticity techniques, economists derive specific prediction for how consumers choose which products to buy, how households save, how firms invest, how workers search for jobs, as well as for how these actions depend on the particulars. They can help them to predict job and consumption behaviours more accurate, it depends on whether the situation is right, such as both competition firms participate to advertise their products in the same time case, it is not right to apply above economic principle to predict consumer behaviours. They will get wrong prediction when they apply this principle to predict consumer behaviours.

However, demand and supply principle can predict below any one of these cases. I shall indicate as below:

The problem of need-based scholarships: Most systems for providing college scholarships are based on some definition of financial needs, with scholarships generally being given only to those students who must need financial help in order to attend school.

Is need, rather than academic ability, the best basic on which to choose those students who are to be encouraged to attend college? Which way of choosing who gets aids is the more just? Which is the more efficient ? Is the overall educational level of society increased more by giving financial aid to bright students or to needy students?

Presumably the aid offers more leverage to needy students, since they all need the money in order to attend college, whereas, many of the bright students would attend college in any case. But is a smaller number of bright students the more important addition?

So, the school can apply demand and supply principle to predict whether how many parents feel need financial assistance and evaluate how much financial amount is the right to borrow. It aims to calculate how many parents feel real financial need and how much to lend to them in order to let these students to get the most fair financial assistance.

Assuming the school wish to use need as a basis, how does the school determines " financial need"?

Is need a function or parents' income? What, then , does the school about children of wealthy parents who are living independently of them and get no aid from parents? Should they be punished for their parents' wealth? But if they are given aid, won't all students, in order to get aid, claim to be independent of their parents?

Is need solely a matter of family income, or should not the school takes a family's financial obligations into account? Does not it make more sense to give aid to someone whose parents must put night more children through school than to someone from a family of five or one only with the same income? But in a possible parallel situations, should a family that carries mortgages on one or two large homes get preference simply because they do not have much money left to spend on college? Does doing this reward ? Is there a difference between the case of night children and the case of the large mortgage? How should parents who are not married , but are living together and supporting their children jointly be counted? Most parents are supporter to their children , although they are married in possible.

So, the school needs to gather all these data to evaluate how many parents are not married or married or living with their children together, how much salary they earn as well as every family has how much children as well as whether they have mortgage for their houses. So, these number will be the financial education assistance demanders, but it does not represent their real financial needs. It is possible that someone does not feel any financial need, although their children apply financial assistance to your school. Then , your school needs to evaluate whether how much financial assistance can lend to every real financial need student family. It can not exceed your final financial expenditure budget (supply) , when your financial expenditure is not enough. SO, demand and supply principle can be applied to research this school real family financial demand to lend to the real financial need families and evaluate whether the reasonable financial amount to lend to every child family to study in your school.

● Supply and demand principle applies to immigration to decide wage case

A fascinating and important example of supply and demand, full of complexities, is the role of immigration in determining wages. If you ask people , they are likely to tell you that immigration into California or Florida US, surely lowers the wages of people in those regions. It is just supply and demand analysis of immigration. According to this analysis, of these to these two regions in US. Immigration in to a region shifts the supply curve for labor to the right and pushes down wages. Why has it relationship between immigration to US these two regions immigrant number and wage? Careful economic studies cast doubt on this simple proposition, however, a recent survey of the evidence concludes:

The effect of immigration on the labor market outcomes of natives is small in US. There is no evidence of economically significant reductions in native employment. Most analysis, finds that a 10 percent increase in the fraction of immigrants in the population reduced native wages by a most 1%.

How can we explain the small impact of immigration on wages? The main mistake is to forget how mobile the American population is and that the impact of immigration on wages, we must examine the effect of new immigrants when the strength of the local economy and the number of native-born residents in a city are unchanged, that is , when these other things are held constant. Unless you exclude the effects other changing variables, you can not accurately predict the impact of immigration. The same principle holds in doing a supply0and demand analysis of any market. As much as possible, when you are examining the impact of a supply or demand shift, you must try to keep all other things constant.

● Rationing by prices

By determining the equilibrium prices and quantities of all inputs and outputs, the market allocated or rations out the scare goods of the society among the possible uses. Who does the rationing? A planning board? Congress or the president? BO, the marketplace, through the interaction of supply and demand, doe the rationing. This is rationing by the purse.

What foods are produces? This is answered by the signals of the market price. High oil prices stimulates oil production, whereas low food prices drive resources out of agriculture. Those who have the most dollars votes have the greatest influences on what goods are produced. All of these considers how demand and supply to the market.

For whom are goods produces? The power of the pursue indicates the distribution of income and consumption. Those with higher incomes end up with larger houses, more clothing, and linger vacations. When the most urgently felt needs get fulfilled through the demand curve.

Even, the how question is decided by supply and demand. When corn prices are low, it is not profitable for farmers to use expensive tractors and irrigation systems, and only the best land is cultivated. When oil prices are high, oil companies drill in deep offshore waters and employ novel seismic techniques to find oil.

IN sum , any thing needs through demands, interact with costs of goods, as reflected in supplies in our economic world. Hence, demand and supply theory ought be the most accurate method to help any businesses or governments to predict their shareholders behaviours when they will change as well as how and how their behaviours change.

Consumer choice theory solves consumer problems in high technological cultural development countries

What is 'consumer choice theory'?

'Consumer choice theory' is a hypothesis about why people buy things. Put simply, it says that you choose to buy the things that give you the greatest satisfaction, while keeping within your budget. At the heart of this theory are three assumptions about human nature.[1] The first assumption is that when you shop, you choose to buy things based on calculated decisions about what will make you happiest. In economics language, this is known as utility maximisation (Economists really like to put quite simple concepts into long complicated terms.)

Secondly, the theory assumes that no matter how much you shop, you will never be completely satisfied. In other words, you will always be happier consuming a little bit more. This is known as the principle of non-satiation.

Thirdly, even though you always get more happiness from more consumption, the amount of pleasure you get from each good decreases with the more you consume. So if you eat two ice creams rather than one, you get more overall pleasure, but the second ice-cream won't be as satisfying as the first. This is known as decreasing marginal utility.

Consumer choice theory has influenced everything from government policy to corporate advertising to academia. But the theory has been criticized for not being the most accurate description of how people actually make choices. A whole new branch of economics, called 'behavioral economics', has emerged essentially to use findings from psychology to disprove the assumptions behind consumer choice theory. This has also led others to argue that consumer choice theory is less about describing how we do actually behave, and is more about describing how people should behave.[3] In other words, by portraying people as self-interested shopaholics, economists are saying that is it okay and natural for us to be avid consumers.

● Consumer choice theory can be applied to solve consumer problems during the country can have economic growth , the reasons may include as below:

The scenario leading to inflation starts with poor growth. Forget about everything that comes next and focus on that most important factor. Because it happens that the scenario leading to a budget crisis also starts with poor growth, and the scenario leading to a long-term unemployment crisis starts with poor growth, and a scenario leading to a better-the-neighbor trade crisis starts with poor growth, and so on. So a very important question is: what can be done to improve the prospects for economic growth? In particular, what is the right countercyclical approach to take to best situate the economy for future growth? I shall indicate during US, America's economy growth occurs, then economists can attempt to apply customer choice theory to solve US itself country's consumer problems more easier.

In no small part, the question comes down to interpretations of charts like the one at right. On the one hand, long and deep downturns seem to have almost no effect on the long-term rate of growth. On the other hand, in the long run we're all dead, and those who live during an extended period of economic weakness suffer for it. Meanwhile, it's also difficult to see where high debt levels influence the long-run rate of growth, at least where this chart is concerned.

During to the medium-term growth stage, is the bigger threat to American growth rates a market revolt against American debt levels? Or is it structural unemployment stemming from the slow, jobless recovery? Or is the cyclical shortfall in public investment? Or something else entirely? Of course, there's no real reason one has to choose a problem to address at the expense of others. More aggressive monetary expansion could make the finding of a solution to all these problems easier, but the Fed is unwilling to oblige me on this score. It may well be concerned that lack of fiscal discipline will lead to increasing inflation expectations, making its job harder (but then fiscal problems are trace able to growth). If that is the worry, however, one has to ask why the Congress has been unable to strike a deal for $20 billion in stimulus this year for $80 billion in fiscal tightening in a year or two (fill in whatever amounts you wish). But the outlook for the American economy vis-a-vis any number of potential crises will hinge on growth, and growth will hinge on the ability of private business to exploit promising opportunities as they arise. And the question is: what's likely to hurt that ability most? High interest rates? Lack of consumer demand? A shortage of adequately prepared workers? Right now firms appear to be most worried about demand shortfalls. So how much can you boost demand without making the primary fear high interest rates? A lot, if the expansion is on the monetary side.

● How to supply consumer choice theory to predict Consumer Behavior Marketing at Apple Computer

During US economy growth, Apply computer applies consumer choice theory to solve its computer buyers' choice problems among different kinds of brand computer competitors. Have you ever wondered why Apple is so successful? They were not the first company to invent the personal computer, portable music device, the tablet, the smartphone, software to download music, or the set-top box to name a few. Apple has amassed a brand loyal following like no other brand backed by significant sales, market share, and profitability. So, how does Apple do it? What's the secret behind their success?

Marketing using consumer behavior insight is how Apple succeeds. Even though Steve Jobs and Apple, did not use consumer research in the initial development of most products, consumer behavior plays a huge role in their marketing and ultimately the success of the company. Once a consumer purchases a product or downloads iTunes Apple has access to data the company leverages. Apple uses this information to gain significant insight into the consumer and what drives purchase behavior.

Consumer behavior marketing is an essential ingredient in the current business climate. The companies that apply this type of marketing well have a distinct competitive advantage that distances them from their rivals. Consumer behavior research is the primary driver at the core of any good strategy. Research provides actionable insight and ensures business success.

If you answer no to the following questions, this post is for you?

•Are you applying consumer behavior marketing currently?

•Have you conducted consumer behavior research within the last two years?

•Do you have consumer behavior marketing in your marketing plan with well-defined marketing strategies and tactics?

•Are you achieving the maximum results for your organization?

Every business has a target audience and consumer behavior marketing provides the fundamental methods for understanding your target. Consumer behavior research provides the underlying element that drives quality strategies and ensures business results.

"Marketing is understanding your buyers really, really well. Then creating valuable products, services, and information especially for them to help solve their problems."

The organizations that have an intimate understanding of their target audience possess a competitive advantage over those that do not. Establishing a one-to-one relationship and thorough knowledge of your target audience is a core responsibility for business in the 21st century and beyond. Regardless if you are B2B, B2C, B2G or a hybrid organization you have a target audience. The information in this post can be applied to any business type. This post focuses on Apple (B2C) employing consumer behavior marketing as a critical ingredient for their success.

Hence, Apply computer shops have several computer teachers to teach any visitors how to use its laptops, hen they enquire its any computer salespeople. Due to its salespeople had been trained to learn how to use the different kinds of laptops. So, anyone enquires them, they can answer their enquires concern any computer questions immediately. Then, they will feel Apple laptops are the first choice to compare other kinds of laptops brands. It is one salespeople answering strategies to persuade any Apple computer visitors to feel its any laptops are the first or preference choice to compare its competitors in this computer market, so customer choice economic theory is the most suitable strategy to solve Apple computer's customer individual purchase decision problem.

Microeconomics Models and Theories solve customer problems

Microeconomics is concerned with the economic decisions and actions of individuals and firms. Within the broad church of microeconomics, there are different theories that certain assumptions and expectations of economic behaviour. The most important theory is neo-classical theory, which places emphasis on free-markets and the assumption individuals are rational and seek to maximise utility. However, there are many critiques of the neo-classical model, arguing economics is more complex with issues of market failure and irrational behaviour.

Pre-classical microeconomic theory

Before, Adam Smith, economics was more disparate with no commanding overall theory. Philosophers like Aristotle and Plato made references to issues in economics such as division of labour. The dominant ideas, pre-classical economics, were based on theories of mercantilism – the idea a nation should try to accumulate gold.

Classical microeconomic theory

Classical microeconomic theory was developed by Adam Smith (Wealth of Nations, 1776) and later economists, such as David Ricardo The essential aspect of classical microeconomic theory include:

Adam Smith mentioned the 'invisible hand of the market.' He noted how when people act out of self-interest, markets tend to provide goods and services which are demanded by the population. It needed no central price setting, but market forces responded to changes in demand and supply, e.g. a shortage pushes up the price and causes demand to fall.

Smith also investigated topics such as the division of labour, specialisation and economies of scale. The early classical economists emphasised the importance of costs to firms and consumers.

Utility maximisation

An important development of classical economics towards the end of the nineteenth century is the concept of utility maximisation. The concept of utility was developed by philosophers/economists – Jeremy Bentham and John Stuart Mill. In microeconomic theory, it was believed a consumer will buy goods depending on the marginal utility (satisfaction) they get from the good. This theory assumes consumers are rational and seeking to maximise the satisfaction they get.

Neo-classical theory

Neo-classical theory is a modern re-interpretation of classical economics of the nineteenth century. Neo-classical theory places importance on markets, but developed new ideas, especially regarding utility and rational choice theory. Elements of neo-classical theory.

1. Market distribution of goods and services.

2.R ational choice theory. This is the idea individuals hold rational preferences and make rational choices; seeking to maximise their outcomes – be it profit, wages, consumption or investment.

3. People act independently and make use of available information.

4. Marginalism. In neo-classical economics, more emphasis was placed on concepts of marginal utility and marginal cost. We make choices depending on satisfaction we get from one extra unit of a good.

Economists such as Carl Menger, William Stanley Jevons and Marie-Esprit-Léon Walras. and Alfred Marshall developed ideas such as diminishing marginal utility. Many of these neo-classical economic theories were brought together in Alfred Marshall's very influential textbook, Principles of Economics. (1890)

•Note there is some blurring between classical economics and neo-classical economics.

•Neo-classical economics has also come to mean 'orthodox economic theory. To a large extent, it has incorporated new developments in microeconomics, such as theories of market failure, market structure and econometrics.

Theories of Market failure

Neo-classical economics has become associated with a belief in the efficiency of markets. However, microeconomic theory has also incorporated the criticisms and limitations of free-markets.

•Monopoly. Adam Smith was well aware of the problem of monopolies and how firms could use their market power to set excessive prices.

•Imperfect competition. In the 1930s, Joan Robinson developed a model of imperfect competition, an awareness many markets were somewhere between monopoly and perfect competition often assumed in neo-classical economics.

•Externalities. Developed by Arthur C.Pigou in The Economics of Welfare (1920) this is the awareness production and consumption decisions can have harmful (or positive) effects on third parties. Therefore, a free market can lead to overconsumption of demerit goods and negative externalities.

•Game theory. An awareness, decisions are not linear or simple, but the interdependence of agents influences what we decide to do.

Behavioural economics

The most important trend in recent decades in economics is the greater emphasis placed on aspects of behavioural economics, which uses many insights from related fields such as psychology.

•Disputes rational choice theory. The essential element of behavioural economics is that it argues individual agents are often not rational and often do not seek to maximise utility.

•Behavioural economics examines how agents can be influenced by biases, and make decisions not predicted by neo-classical economic theory. Behavioural economics can explain the irrational exuberance of booms and busts.

Econometrics

In the post-war period, economics became increasingly mathematical with economists attempting to use mathematics to explain models and theories. Econometrics looks at economic data and seeks to extract simple relationships. The basic tool is the linear regression models and can be used to try and predict consumer spending and demand for labour.

Heterodox models of microeconomics

Heterodox models differ substantially from microeconomic foundations of neo-classical economics. Schools of thought include

Marxist economic theory

Karl Marx developed an alternative perspective on economics. He focused on the surplus value created under the capitalist economic system. To Marx, the invisible hand of the market would be better described as the invisible hand of capitalist exploitation of workers. Marx claimed workers did receive their full labour value but were compensated for their necessary labour only – enabling capitalists to profit from the surplus.

Institutional economics. The role of society and institutions in shaping economic behaviour. For example, Thomas Veblen looked at theories of 'conspicuous consumption' and noted how the desire for social status could drive much economic theory. Institutional economics could be seen as a forerunner for later behavioural economics.

Environmental economics Argues traditional economics wrongly places value on increasing output. The most important thing is creating a sustainable environment which maximises living standards. So, manufacturers need to consider how to manufacture their products , but pollution can not be raised as the same time, because human will face to raise cost of living and living experiences to be poor , even food shortage, water pollution , air pollution , death rate raises when technological productivities brings pollution to our natural environment. Hence, environmental economoic theory is the most suitable to solve manufacturers' pollution problem.

Buddhist economics/non-profit goals. Like environmental economics, this questions the assumption higher incomes and higher output are desirable. The theory of hedonistic relativism suggests higher incomes do nothing to increase happiness levels, and traditional economics can encourage society to pursue materialistic goals which actually create more problems of stress, conflict and environmental degradation.

Some of the basic models you might find in A-Level economics :

•Price Discrimination

•Perfect competition

•Price Mechanism

•Monopoly

•Oligopoly and kinked demand curve

•Game Theory Pricing strategies

•Market failure

•Behavioural economics

ON conclusion, any macro economy theories can be applied to find the most reasonable methods to solve any customer problems in societies by economists as above. So, I believe that any economic and customer and social problems can be solved by economic theories in our society.

Demand and supply theory solves social problems

Over the past 20 years, many researchers believe to apply behavioral economic macroeconomic models which can predict market behavioral change. The reasons are based on assumptions of optimizing behavior in many cases have difficulty accounting for key real-world observations. Hence, researchers have used behavioral economics assumptions with the aim of making their model predicting better fit the data. The reason for behavioral economics results into macroeconomics will be more accurate to predict market behavioral change in macro-economy view point, such as economic fluctuation prediction, the consumption, formation of expectations and determination of wages and employment how to aggregation supply and the possibility of consumer individual demand product or service number prediction more accurately.

● How to apply behavioral economy (demand and supply) theory to predict marketing behavioral changes more accurate?

Anyway, economists aim to develop models of human behavior and interactions in market in order to build useful models. Economists make simplifying assumptions to analyze why the market will be changed by consumer individual consumption behavior changing. Why do I assume consumers are as economic man ? In behavioral economy view point, how the perception of the economic man's behavior (including consumer choices) of economic models with the development of economics as a science. Economists explain the concept of economics as a science. It is the concept of consumer as an economic man, the essence and complexity of consumer behavior.

The consumer and consumer purchasing behavior are an important area of interest of many scientific disciplines. The process of economic decision making as well as consumption choices are connected with wider human activities. The terms of both consumer individual attitudes and group social behavior will influence group social behavior will influence consumer individual final consumption decision in every consumption choice process. Thus, behavioral economy method can predict consumer behavioral changing, it can apply these sciences to research, includes sociology, psychology, anthropology, operational research, decision theory etc. different literature research aspects. I assume that businessmen can apply behavioral economy method to predict market changing behaviors successfully if they own behavioral economy knowledge.

In this part, I shall concentrate on explain how the perception of the economic man's behavior (including consumer choice) is applied to predict market behaviors. After explaining the concept of consumer as an economic man, the nature and complexity of consumer behavior are discussed to below different industries' marketing behavioral changing every case studies in US or UK countries.

Why is consumer as an economic man? IN behavioral economy

view point, the concept of answer is one of the fundamental concepts in economics because the consumer is the case market participant along with the producer. In general, lecturers define the consumer in various ways, but in behavioral economy view point, consumers mean economy man. Because who will compare cost and benefit to any product or service to decide to choose to buy the product or consume the service. Consumers are as "economic man", who will make own subjective preferences (tastes), habits and traditions and existing objective constraints (i.e. disposal income) market prices of products and services in order to satisfy whose needs to a maximum degree and in the most rational way.

Thus, economic man means consumers need to make psychological mind to decide whether who either prefer to buy this product or another product or prefer to consume this service or another service more suitable. Thus, any markets or industries need have themselves benefits and consumers must need to evaluate whether the product or service has more benefits to compare other products or services in the consumption market to satisfy whose needs. It means that if the product or service has more benefits to compare other similar products or services. Then the product or service will persuade many consumers to choose to but the product or consume the service.

Consequently, in first part, I shall indicate how to apply behavioral economy theory : economic man psychological method, benefits and costs benefits method, how to predict these US and UK enterprises marketing behavioral changing more accurate.

In the second part, I shall apply micro employee behavioral economy concept to explain how to solve these US and UK inter-organizational management challenge.

I believe that behavioral economy method can be applied to research organizational employee behaviors change, e.g. how any why the employee chooses to do this action in whose organization. Moreover, behavioral economy method can be applied to consumption market to predict how any why the consumer choose to buy the product or consume the service. So, any consumers and employees personal psychology and external environment economic factor will influence how to choose to do decision in any organizations or consumption environment.

Bibliography

Bandiera, O., I. Barankay, and I. Rasul (2005). Social preferences and the response to incentives: Evidence from personal data. The quarterly journal of economics 120 (3), 917-969.

Exadaktylos, F., A.M. Espin and P. Branas-Garza (2013). Experimental subjects are not different. Scientific reports 3, 1213.

Lazear, E.P. (1979). Why is there mandatory retirement? Journal of political economy 87(6), 1261-1284.

● Behavioral economic method (demand and supply theory) predicts stable basic income consumer individual spending behavior in high technological cultural countries

Can apply behavioral economic method to predict that the consequences of a stable basic income consumer's consumption behavior? It may be significantly different than the ones are predicted by the standard economic model if more realistic assumptions of human consumption behavioral prediction success.

Behavioral economic method assumes that consumer will compare whether whose benefits are more than costs after they buy the product or consume the service. I assume the consumer is only the who have stable basic income source consumer target. This stable basic income target consumers who will evaluate or feel they will earn more benefits than costs to every product in their consumption process, after they will make final decision to choose to buy the product to use or consume the service. Otherwise, if they feel they won't earn more benefits after they buy the product or consume the service in the consumption process. Then, they won't choose to buy the product to use or consume the service. In behavioral economic view point, it indicates their consumption behaviors are depend on comparing the product or the service whether it can satisfy their desire benefits and their desire benefits to the product or service must be more than their consumption cost.

There are four points to apply behavioral economic method to predict each stable basic income individual income spending. They include: motivation, conspicuous consumption, social preferences and crowding theory.

Each stable basic income consumer individual spending amount will be different and it is represent that every high stable basic income consumer must decide to consume any high cost services or buy high cost products to use. Although some economic teachers assume general high income people will accept to spend more expenditures for enjoyment or buy high cost of products to satisfy basic high level necessary expenditures. But, applying behavioral economic analysis, it is not absolute true, some low income people also accept to spend more to buy high cost of products or increasing spending expenditures for enjoyment for their basic necessary expenditures.

The field of behavioral economic can be fined as a combination of economics and psychology that tries to capture human behavior in a more realistic. Understanding each consumer individual consumption behavior, we need to know how who does each decision to influence each consumption choice. Consequently, analysis reaches the conclusion. Every high or low level stable basic income consumer individual behavioral consumption that the microeconomic consequences of a stable basic income of individual consumer target consumption group could be efficiency enhancing, but at the same time incentives about positional concerns could lead to wasteful and inefficient spending to the stable low basic income consumer target group.

● How to apply demand and supply theory to contribute to the stable basic income target consumer group's consumption prediction?

What is basic income mean? A basic income is an income paid by a political community to all its members on an individual basis, without means test or work requirement. How to apply behavioral economic method to contribute to the basic income consumption prediction?

I assume high income tax is charged to one high income tax payee , it will influence the high income tax payee individual consumption desires to be fallen, also extrinsic incentives will effort and intrinsic motivation and how the labor market change these variables under and big changes predicting, how income security changes social consumption preferences, e.g. how a big change affects the overall level of status -seeking behavior and this effect with income inequality to influence consumer individual consumption attitude or habit.

How can behavioral economic methods predict consumer's consumption decision, in special the stable basic income consumer target group? In any consumption decisions are involving risk and uncertainty, the standard economic model usually assumes that decisions are based on final condition, regardless of the changes are caused by the results of a consumer's decision.

An alterative mode of how consumers make decision and judgement under risk and uncertainty. This situation is often occurred in consumption market.

In behavioral economic view point, it explains how consumer's consumption, however, which excludes the stable basic income earn factor can influence the stable basic income earn target consumer group decides to make final consumption decision to compare to the non-stable basic income earn target consumer group. The reasons include as below:

(1) Consumers evaluate decisions over gains and losses with respect to some natural reference point, when they feel need to consume, which is assumed to be judgement about a sequence of outcomes are based on changes in wealth, rather than whether how much absolute basic income earn to influence whose consumption desires.

(2) Thus, behavioral economic theory assumes the consumer is the low level of income group in society, but when who feels that he is still gains more than losses when who decides to buy the expensive product or consumes the expensive service. Then, the

low level of income consumer who will accept to buy the expensive product or consume the service easily. Due to whose gains feeling is more than losses feeling, when who buys the product or consumes the service.

(3) Behavioral economic theory also assumes the taxpayer will pay high income tax in this year. The, even the high income taxpayer can earn high basic income, but due to whom needs to pay high income tax in this year. Then, he/she will reduce much spending, even he/she reduces spending on cheap products or cheap service consumption for enjoyment. This is the taxpayer's economic decision to influence whose consumption behavior, due to the high income tax expenditure factor influences whose consumption behavior to change to be reduced spending expenditures in this year.

How to apply behavioral economic method to predict labor market changing behavior?

Instead of applying behavioral economic method to predict every consumer individual consumption effort. Behavioral economic method can be also be applied to predict every country's labor market changing behavior. Particularly, how salary clerical workers or low wage labor workers should move from one type of job to another based on these factors. They include as below:

Their intrinsic motivation and how their levels of effort would change after this movement, investigates the effects of income security on social preferences in labor market changing behavior, and how cooperation in social contribution is affected when income security is guaranteed, how to predict the role of positional externalities on conspicuous consumption and how would change the incentive to influence consumption. So, it seems that general labor market job changing behaviors will not influenced by external economic environment better or worse changing factor, or salary changing factor etc. different environmental condition changing factors influence to employees' job changing. Generally, employee's job changing behavior is more influenced to persuade who changes job by himself/herself intrinsic motivation negative emotion influence mainly.

How to apply motivation crowding theory to predict labor productivity? One of the main challenges of economic theory is to find what are the optimal incentives that increase productivity of labors. The standing point is usually extrinsic incentive be it is form of monetary compensations for high effort or fine for low effort.

It is a kind method of reward or punishment to increase or decrease number of productivity to every labor. But it can only raise short term number of productivity in possible and it can not guarantee high quality of productivity. So if one employer wants a labor to do more of an activity or with a higher quality, consider paying the labor for working hard on punishing whom if for providing a low level effort.

This idea is that people do not like to work, and therefore they used some sort of compensation for doing a specific activity, and that the more they are paid the harder, they will work. So, payment better compensation is only beneficial to encourage labors to do one specific task or activity in short term. This method can not be suitable to rise long term beneficial productivity and high level quality of production or excellent performance in long term and it can only keep in short term raising productivity and high level quality of production or excellent performance benefits.

Consider paying the labor for working hard on punishing whom if for providing a low level effort. This idea is that people do not like to work, and therefore they used some sort of compensation for doing a specific activity, and that the more they are paid the harder they will work. So, payment better compensation is only beneficial to encourage labors to do one specific task or activity in short term. This method can not be suitable to raise long them beneficial productivity and high quality of products.

However, economists would argue that, is a labor has high intrinsic motivative to perform a task, who will provide a high level of effort without compensation by himself/herself but an even higher level of effort of whom is compensated. If a labor does not have any intrinsic motivation to perform a task or an activity, who will provide no effort or a low effort of whom. There is no compensation, but who will increase this level of effort of an extrinsic incentive is implemented.

Hence, in behavioral economic view point, the labor individual high level effort is a main psychological factor to influence whose productivity to be raised or the qualities of products to be raised, when the products are manufactured by the high level effort labor. It means that high compensation is not the good method to encourage labor productivity or raise quality. Otherwise, how to influence the one low level of effort of labor to change to be one high level of effort labor. It is the best psychological method to influence the labor to raise productivity and quality and service performance to any products or services in manufacturing process or service process for any organizations in long term beneficial possible.

● How can apply demand and supply theory raises basic stable income consumer consumption desire

Economists aim to develop models of human behavior and interactions in consumption markets. But consumers behave in complex ways, such as how to predict consumers to make rational decisions in consumption processes. Moreover, self-consumption control and motivation can vary significantly across different individual consumer.

In order to build useful consumption prediction models, economists make simplifying assumptions, aims to predict how to raise stable basic income consumer target group consumption more success. However, behavioral economy method is one kind of accurate consumption prediction method. It can be applied to predict economic decision-making to every consumer consumption choice more accurate raising whose consumption desire?

I shall indicate how to apply different behavioral economy methods (demand and supply theory) to raise stable basic stable income target consumer group consumption desire in these different consumption situation (consumption environment) aspects as below:

1. Stable basic stable income consumer group consumption great or small amount desire

The consumption of products and services is a fundamental part of consumer's welfare. Basically, every one who has stable basic stable income, who will like to consume any products and services. Even, consumption great or small amount desire won't be depended on whether the person whose income is more or less. It means low income level of people will still like to consume great amount to buy expensive products or consume expensive services, because consumption is human's part of life and basic needs.

This stable basic income people will like to consume, because they have stable income source when they do not worry about unemployment occurrence to cause them have no enough money to support their life. Otherwise, non-stable basic stable income people won't like to consume because they feel they have no stable basic income source to support their life and they will worry about unemployment occurrence any time. Hence, stable basic income people will have more consumption desire to compare non-stable basic stable income people in any countries usually. Behavioral economic method indicates they feel their economic benefits will be loss if they planned to buy any products or consume any services easily. So, they prefer to save money in bank more than consumption.

1. Demand systems and micro-economic factor influence basic income people consumption attitude

Why stable basic income people will like to consume? Because who have more demand, a demand system shows the level of consumer demand for different products and services: e.g. one basic stable income person may refer to the demand for clothes, another the demand for food etc.

How the demand for that particular product varies with the prices and demographic factor will influence who to accept consumption. Such as stable basic income people who will not consider to decide to buy the cloth to wear or the food to eat if who feel the cloth or food price is even more expensive to compare other kind of cloth or food.

Otherwise, non-stable basic income people who will consider to decide to buy the cloth to wear or the food to eat if they feel that they still have enough cloths to wear or enough food to eat at homes , even these food or cloth price are less expensive to compare others. Because they feel they lack stable income effort to support them to consume. Hence, basic stable income factor can influence the consumer's consumption decision.

2. Life-cycle advertisement method can influence consumer individual consumption behaviors to be increased

Consumer behavior makes strong assumptions about the informational and computational bases of consumer behavior. Generally, consumer behavior is reasonably characterized as the maximization of expected lifetime utility subject to budget constraint and conditional on the available information.

Generally, consumers prefer to buy any discounted products or it is reasonable that consumers accept to buy many attractions to persuade them to buy any kinds of bargain discount products. Hence, low bargain discount product is one good behavioral economic principle to encourage or persuade or attract any consumers to increase consumption.

What is behavioral life-cycle model? This model explains consumer behavior can be persuaded to buy any discounted products by advertisement, e.g. television, radio, newspapers, magazine etc. promotion channels. Because frequent advertisement promotion method can let any consumers often remember the product's brand, discounted price, style, color and image from advertisement content.

So, advertisement can be one part of consumer behavioral life-cycle. For example, when the television audiences often watch TV. Hence, when the brand of product advertisement often makes fun image and discounted message to let TV audiences to remember this brand of product, when they are watching TV. Then, it has possible to persuade any potential consumers to choose to buy this brand of any products or consume this brand of any services, due to its advertisement of discounted sale message is very attractive to every one to let this advertisement audience's attention to remember this brand of products or services are selling or serving in market at this moment. So, it is advertisement image behavior influences audiences to buy the brand's any products attractively and persuasively.

3. Raising electricity consumption from electricity user individual habit

For electricity use market case example, how to analyze people's behavior in consuming electricity using a behavioral economic framework ? Electricity consumption is modeled by the means of consumer's individual useful habit, electricity price, consumer satisfaction level, willingness to invest in new technologies, social interactions, and marketing strategies by the power utility. Because electricity is necessary to every home or electric vehicle users needs or businessmen office etc. different needs every day.
Power companies supply electricity to a region's homes and industries. However, electricity needs modernization of power system companies expect to increase price. Due to competitive factor, such as other fuel resource choices, outdated kind of energy electricity supply, and renewable fuel energy source competition.
Hence, applying behavioral economic concept, I assume electricity consumers will compare to electricity and other kinds of energy choices to weigh up the costs and benefits of all alternatives, aiming to maximize their benefits, before making a decision to choose to use electricity for their house electricity demand or electric vehicle or shop or factory manufacturing etc. function of different aspects of electricity users.
For example, electricity business clients, they aim to reduce cost, such as energy expenditure, when they use any energy to manufacture their products in factories. If they feel electricity is expensive price to compare other kinds of energy power supply.

When, they feel that they can not earn much beneficial advantages to use electricity to produce their products. Otherwise, if they feel other any kinds of energy supply can replace electricity to give more benefits to compare electricity energy. Then, many business electricity users will change to use other kinds of energies to consume to replace electricity power.

However, electricity can have competitive ability in electric vehicles market, if many drivers feel environment protection is more important to compare vehicles will be popular to be driven, due to many drivers don't want air pollution. They will like gas vehicles. Hence, the main attribute from the consumer side is one their habit electricity consumption behaviors, satisfaction level, energy efficient interaction with the power utility.

Consequently how to predict electricity consumer's demand. The important factor is how to let electricity users to feel power companies are changing a reasonable level to compare other similar energy supply products. When electricity users feel electricity which can bring more benefits to compare other kinds of energy products. Then, in energy supply market, if the demanding number of electricity consumers can increase more than other kinds of energy demanding number. Then, it is right time to raise electricity price to charge electricity consumers. Hence, how to persuade electricity consumers to feel that they can have more benefits to compare other kinds of energy products. It is the main successful factor to electricity power supply companies.

● Consumer confidence is as a predictor of consumption spending

Behavioral economists believe it has link between confidence and economic decisions to cause consumers to choose spending, if the consumer has confidence to believe the product is worth to use, then who will accept to buy the product to use.

Concentrated on the conceptualization of confidence and its role in mode in theories of consumption. It also concerns on whether the confidence indicators contain any information beyond economic fundamentals. The concern is whether confidence can be explained by current and past value of variables, such as income, unemployment, inflation or consumption or in other way.

Whether confidence measures have any statistical significance in predicting economic outcomes once information from the above variables is used. Economic variable factor will also influence consumer confidence to decide consumption spending, e.g. real consumption expenditures (income, wealth or interest rate).

Finally, it will identify under which circumstances confidence indicates can be a good predictor of household consumption. Hence, survey is one good measurement method to predict whether how much every household has confidence to spend to consume the brand of products to use. Why is survey a good confidence consumption measurement prediction to every household in every country?

The reasons include survey can gather every household consumption habit history data to evaluate whether every survey person has how much confidence to consume the brand of products. Which in most cases correspond to periods where there are large changes in household survey indicators, liking during financial crises or geopolitical tensions to measure or predict whether the country's future good or bad economic condition factor will influence every household consumption desire in the year.

This modelling approach assumes that there is a certain (unknown) in confidence index changes beyond which confidence starts impacting consumption behaviors. So, sample household surveys can show the contribution of confidence in explaining consumption expenditures increases when household survey indicators feature large changes. So that confidence indicators can have some increasing predictive power during the survey investigation period in the year.

Other view point, surveys have been concerned on whether the confidence indicators contain any information beyond economic fundaments. The concern is whether confidence can be explained by current and past values of variables, such as income, unemployment, inflation or consumption or the other way. Whether confidence measures have any statistical significance in predicting economic outcomes once information from different external variable factors to influence the survey household group.

What is confidence in consumption survey ?

Confidence in consumption. For example, to measure whether how much degree of strong inflation in the economy, such as recessions and recoveries will influence the country's household confident consumption in the year.

The surveys consumers' questions usually concern on major expenditures and changes in the respondent's financial situation, focus on job availability and current business conditions etc. questions. It is then possible that about consumer confidence depending on the relative performance of the variables that may be more relevant balances, with respect to the factors that determine unemployment and other labor market related issues. It aims to investigate whether those any one of variable factors will influence consumers general loss confident consumption desire in this year.

What is a confidence indicator ?

A confidence indicator is considered as an explanatory variable for consumption together with standard variables used on predicting consumption expenditure. However, the natural real personal consumption expenditure is unexpected and unpredicted easily.

In conclusion, consumption expenditure depends the consumer individual confidence. If the consumer has much confidence to feel this year economic change will be better and he/she is easily to find job, then he/she will accept consumption easily in this year. It seems financial wealth and unemployment etc. economic factors will influence every household consumption desire. So, survey is one kind of good psychological consumption prediction method to predict consumption spending for any country in the year. I recommend manufacturers may choose to apply survey method to attempt to enquire sample survey people to gather data to predict whether what degree of consumption desire to them and find solution methods to solve low degree of consumption desire challenge.

How to apply behavioral economy methods to influence employee individual psychology to achieve raise productivity of long term incentive intention?

Increasing salary is short term incentive productivity method. Behavioral economy assumes labors will choose to do beneficial behaviors to themselves when they feel their work behaviors can earn more benefits to themselves more than their employers in the organizations. Otherwise, if they feel their work behaviors can earn more benefits to their employers more than themselves. Then, they won't choose to do their work behaviors, e.g. raising productivities or work hard. Due to they feel work hard or raise productivities behaviors that only give more benefits to their employers more themselves.

Whether does cheap product price incentive consumption desire to influence effective consumption behavior? Whether is monetary increasing salary payment incentive labors might be willing to work on task? I feel raising labors productivities is similar to raise incentive consumption, which both have similar point, such as increasing salary payment or cheap product price is the main factor to influence incentive consumption or raising productivities. Hence, it seems monetary factor is not the main effort to encourage labors to work hard.

In labor's behavioral economic view point, for example, if an employer pays an employee more doing a task, who might be less willing to work on it, who might be less productive given whose efforts and who may enjoy the task less. If you want your employees to save more for retirement. You may want to give them fewer investment options. If you want them to engage more in a task, you might want offer them an additional alternative, instead of increasing salary to that task. Thus, increasing salary is not only method to encourage productivities of incentives.

How to improve the design of incentive structures to encourage productivities in any organizations?

Any monetary incentive can only encourage productivities in short term. It can not only encourage productivities in long term in any organizations. It is similar to cheap or discount product price can only attractive consumers to buy the product in short term, it can not attract consumers to choose to buy the product in long term, it prefers to have more options to encourage labors to incentive productivities, e.g. investing good beneficial retirement plans. Suggesting that employees do not have free disposal of their investment options. These standard incentives seem irrelevant raising salary monetary factor, they can be quite effective in inducing labors to take particular actions to incentive productivities in long term. Due to when they can hard work, then they have more beneficial retirement plans or investing plans for their retirement. It means when they can achieve the most effective or efficient productivities to the employer for long term. It will give better retirement benefits and investment benefits to the better or even the best performance of employees. Otherwise, the worst performance employees won't earn good retirement benefits and investment benefits, when their employers feel their perform very poor in the organizations in long term.

Hence, increasing salary level method is not one successful long term incentive method to persuade every employee to raise productivities or encourage excellent performance optional method. Increasing salary level is only similar to reduce product price and it is only short term encouragement to consumption or productivities method.

In conclusion, extrinsic monetary factor can not incentive labor's raising productivities more than every employee themselves intrinsic motivation to raise productivities as excellent performance in any organizations. Thus, organizations need to let employees to feel that they can give long term economic benefits to encourage their intrinsic motivation effort to be raised their productivities or performance more effective or efficient in order to achieve long term both win-win economic benefits to employees and employers both.

Building employees and managers kindly co-operational relationship method

If you are an economist, your employer has no without any financial incentive to encourage your economic research tasks in your organization. It is equally difficult to certify that such activity will contribute to your growth of human capital and increased productivity in research or teaching.

The standard model, which explains employee's effort only through the way (determined by productivity), is therefore incomplete. In particular, it doesn't consider that incentives to work do not have to be monetary in other words, that there are other things besides the disutility of labor (Kamenica, 2012) and section 1.3 have.

Why will short term wage increasing method only influence short term labor supply to raise productivities? The effect of reference raising wage can be most easily identified on short term labor supply to raise productivities. For US, New York city taxi drivers case, they have to decide every day for low long they are going to offer their services, given the day-to-day variable ability of demand they face (peaking during bad weather and/or when big conferences and public events are taking place in the city).

In the standard model, houses worked should grow with any growth in demand for New York taxi drivers' services. (one day's earning will have only a negligible income effect in the longer run). And yet actual cabbies work less on a demand heavy day. One of possible explanations suggests that New York city taxi drivers expect a certain income, they have set themselves a specific target income, who expect to achieve every day. During low demand for their taxi services, then they work longer hours to reach the target, when during peak demand, their referential income is achieved quickly and they only work short hours. Elasticity of hours worked with respect to their earnings is therefore negative (Lamerer, Babcock, Loewenstein, & Thaler, 1997).

However, taxi driver is either one self employment business or one taxi company employment driving service occupation. It is similar to other kinds of service jobs in societies. Servicing employees, such as waiters, salespeople, securities, customer services, bus drivers etc. different kinds of service occupations. They are not similar to manufacturing occupation to be applied how many amount of piece of products production to evaluate their productivities efforts. Thus these any one of service job nature is depended on their service performance to clients to feel their service performances are excellent to compare general service performance effort of service employees.

Considerably, respectively, I assume that if these service employees' managers can build kindly working environment, e.g. manager individual attitude and behavior can let their employees to feel happy to work together in their teams. Then, the managers' kindly as enthusiastic behaviors or attitudes will let every employee more positive encouragement of service attitude to serve their clients in their teams. Then, the client complaining number will be possible reduced, even none of any complains. Hence, building kindly relationship between managers and employees will raise excellent service performance to any organization service nature employees.

Can bonus method encourage service performance to be raised ?

In service job nature of bonus method can also raise employees' overall productivities or service performance. For example, when employees got a provisional bonus before the start of the workweek, but were warned that they would lose it on payday, unless they achieve the productivities or excellent service performance norm, they worked more productivities or let many clients to satisfy their service performance. Hence, managers can achieve bonus plan to compensate any excellent productivity or excellent services to them. Then, they can let clients to feel their service performance more satisfactory than employees of a control group who were merely given the standard promise to receive a bonus upon achieving the norm.

The effort was relatively small, however, productivity grew 1%. Interestingly, the effect of a loss was stronger when how teams were rewarded this way, social pressure came to bear on the less productivity team members. When the team members won't earn any bonus. So, long-term productivity gains were achieved through bonuses paid by excellent performance compensation method to compare to low service performance employees receiving no bonuses at all.

Economic views of human motivation nature

There are only two main types of economic actors and by making simplifying assumptions about how these types of actors behave and interact. The two basic sets of actors in this model are firms, which are assumed in this model are firms, which are assumed to maximize their profits from producing and selling products and services, households, which are assumed to maximize their utility (or satisfaction) from consuming products and services.

It seems any employees will choose to do behaviors to achieve to earn much benefits from their organizations. The models of economic behaviors that consider considerate employees' choice of goals, the actions they take to achieve these goals and the limitations and influences that affect their choices and actions.

For university students choose which universities to study case, suppose that any college enrollment students are deciding which courses to study. Thus, it implies that if the university can provide many different kinds of suitable or right courses to any college enrollment students to choose to study. It means that if the university can provide many different kinds of courses to enrollment students to choose to study. Then, it will have much chance to attract enrollment students to choose this university to study. It's competition can be raised by many courses choice factor. but, in fact, it is not absolute right, although the university can provide many courses to provide to enrollment students to choose to study. But, it is not guarantee to represent it must attract many students to enroll this university to study.

For example, suppose that college enrollment students are deciding which courses to choose to study. Although, it has right course to prepare to these enrollment students to choose to study. But, they see a summary of evaluations from hundreds of other students indicating that a certain course is very good in this university. Then, suppose that they match a video interview of just one student to give a negative review of this university of the course. Even when students were told in advance that such a negative review was worse to this university of the course. They tended to be more influenced by the negative review than the summary of hundreds of evaluations, even although such behavior seems irrational. Hence, although many right courses choice has much chance to attract students to enroll this university to study. But, if its bad educational quality from this course from negative review factor, which will influence the enrollment students number to be reduced.

It implies that students will compare this university's the course educational quality whether is better or worse to compare other universities' similar course educational quality, even this university's this course fee whether is reasonable in educational market. This is cost and beneficial comparison behavioral economy principle to all enrollment students before they decide to choose which universities.

Hence, this case implies that universities how to train teachers' teaching skills to let students to feel that they can learn new knowledge from their teaching staffs absolutely. It means how to raise education training skills to raise teachers' teaching performance. It is very important factor to influence the university's teaching development success. So, many courses choice is not important factor to attract many students to enroll the university. Otherwise, although the university can not provide many courses to let students to enroll, but it's teachers can provide excellent teaching service to teach whose students. This is important factor to attract many students to choose to enroll this university to study.

Under-level productive efficiency and low-consumption desire behavioral economic influences

In behavioral economic influence view point, I feel that under-level productive efficiency is the represent low production number to the manufacturer as well as low-consumption desire is not represent less consumers demands or customers lose confidence to the product.

On the one hand, I shall apply behavioral economic method to analyze why under productive efficiency is not represent low production number influence. Otherwise, I feel under-productive efficiency will have possible to increase production number after the manufacturer can review what factor(s) to influence under-productive efficiency.

I shall give reasons to explain as below:

As Jim, P. & Brendan. M. (2013) indicated who had ever been experiencing failure to do their businesses. Although, they had lost a million dollars, but they felt that they can be taught to learn undiscovered knowledge to know how to do their businesses successful by their wrong judgement and decision learning experience. They explained that " in ll risk taking, speculation, business ventures, entrepreneurial activities, it is the loss side on which you must focus first. This is even true for gambling, the gambler determines how much he's willing to bet, and loss, before the game is played. He doesn't wait for the game to end and then let the croupier or dealer assign his wager for him. How do you determine the downside, and how do you control or minimize it? With objective decision making and a plan that has as its starting point the stop-loss parameters"

Hence, it explains any business will have under-level productive efficiencies and low consumption desire business risk. However, to any one entrepreneur, who needs to know it is one game between the himself/herself and whose clients. They also need to know with objective decision making and a plan that has as its starting point.

Hence, I assume that if the entrepreneur has wrong decision to cause under-level productive efficiency, it is possible that, due to there is no enough employee number to manufacture the product or many employees are not skillful to manufacture all product in normal time or many employees are lazy etc. different factors to cause under-level productivities. However, when they discover their productivities are very low to compare similar competitors their employees' productivities and efficiencies. Then, they can attempt to find what factor(s) to cause low productivities and low efficiencies. it is possible that any one among of these factors case. They include many employees' lazy to influence low productivities or there is no enough employee number or many employees are not skillful to manufacture their products in production process.

Hence, wrong decision or plan is not represent failure. Otherwise, it can give chance to let the entrepreneur to learn whether what the factor(s) is (are) to cause low productivities and low efficiencies in whose product manufacturing process. As I feel that under-level productive efficiency is not represent low production number. Because I assume that if one worker lacks enough skills and manufacturing experiences to manufacture the product, but who can spend less time to manufacture the product and whose spending manufacturing time is same to the another owning enough skillful worker's time to do the product. Hence, I believe that the product quality from the low-skillful worker's manufacturing skill, it's quality will be worse to compare to the product quality from the high skillful worker's manufacturing skill. Hence, if the low skillful worker needs to spend much time to produce the product, but the product quality can be same to the high skillful worker's product quality. It means that it is sure because the low skillful worker has no excellent skill to compare to the high skillful worker to produce the product. Hence, his manufacturing spending time must be longer than the high skillful worker's time. It implies that the low skillful worker spends less time to raises high production number, but his product must be poor quality to sell. Then, his fast and efficient manufacturing speed that is not achieve economic beneficial to the organization's manufacturing process, e.g. less electricity spends to manufacture the product. Otherwise, the low skillful worker's fast and efficient manufacturing speed of behavior will raise the organization's cost in manufacturing process because consumers would not like to choose to buy any low quality product when they can choose which similar products to compare which one has the best quality and cheap price to buy.

Hence, efficient production is not the main factor to influence the business's success. Otherwise, good quality of the product factor is more important to compare it to influence the business's success.

On the other hand, I shall apply behavioral economic theory to analyze why low-consumption desire is not represent consumer demand lose to the business. As Jim. P. & Brendan. M. (2013) also identified " rather than looking for success to follow, who explained the formula for failure to avoid. As an Wang, founder of Wang laboratories said " it is my belief that there are no secret to success." The formula for failure is not lack of knowledge, brains, skills or hard work and it's not lack of luck, it's personalizing losses, especially of preceded by a string of wins or profits. It's refusing to acknowledge and accept the reality of a loss when it starts to occur because to so so would reflect negatively on you."

Thus, as whose feeling to explain why low-consumption desire is not represent less consumers demands or customers lose confidence to the product. The reasons include the causes of low-consumption desire are possible due to worse economic environment factor influences consumption desire to be reduced. It is not due to whether the product price is too high or quality is worse to compare others. Hence, as Jim & Brendan indicated the formula for business failure is not lack of knowledge, brains, skills or hard work and it's not lack of luck. It's not lack of luck. It's personalizing losses, means its reflecting to knowledge and accept the reality of a loss when it starts to occur. As it is applied to explain why low-consumption desire is not represent less consumers demands or customers lose confidence to the product. It's possible that external economic environment changing worse factor to cause the business personalizing losses, it is not reflect who lacks knowledge, skill, hard work factors to cause failure. Hence, ho to predict when and how and why economic environment changes worse will be important factor to predict when and how and why consumption behavioral changes to cause business's success.

● Demand and supply theory solves organizational problems

Any organizations can let salespeople feel happy to sell their products. Then their sale performance will also raise. The question concerns that how to make them to feel happy to help the organization to sell their products? I shall explain some methods as below:

How to manage sales for predictable revenue? In order to hold salespeople sale psychology whether they feel happy or unhappy, executives need to understand the essential activities, sales managers must focus on to be analysts for change, foster continuous improvement and create a sales culture that drives results. Sale executives need to know how to achieve top objectives of sales management is to drive sales, capture new revenue and exceed monthly sales and margin objectives, e.g. performing sale straregy development with each salesperson on Monday morning at a minimum, and in a formal one-on-one meeting during the week;using strategy tools and questioning techniques to ensure the prospects are qualified and the strategy is valid; knowing the ratio between future values and future monthly quotos to raise sale opportunities; six month on-going sale plan aims to make sure there are coordinated to achieve sale to various market segments; developing on ongoing series of networking events to build market awareness in order to ensure all salespeople attend specific events involved in networking by salespeople to, understanding the market how to influence salespeople sale method to sale number, understanding trends and seeking some channels to raise additional sales opportunities; how to create trained or warm sale environment to let sales teams feel happy to sell.

How to design and utilize efficient control sale procedures? The sale cycle procedure may include these market activities, such as advertising, sales promotion, market research, physical distribution, pricing , sale place, sale staffs seeking. SO, any organizations need have good sale planning, direction and control of the personnel, selling activities of a business with including recruiting, selecting, training, rating, supervising, paying or reward system, motivating strategy , as all these tasks apply to the personnel sales-force.

The factors may influence salespeople psychology, they may include fair income reward system, or appreciation methods and sale career development plan to every salesperson. It aims to encourage them to achieve the highest sale effort. Anymore, methods to train sale managers have the right direction to guide, lead and motivate their salespeople, e.g. knowledge of salespeople psychology needs how to satisfy them, understanding why they choose to do or act themselves sale behaviors in order to improve their weakness to motivate salespeople to achieve company's sale target goal every month easily, e.g. raising profitability, sales volume, market share, growth and corporate image building raise clients' confidence to choose to buy this company's any products more easily.

The sales organization is required for the following purposes, they may include: enabling top-management, to devote to more time in policy making for the growth and expansion of business to divide and fix authority among the subordinates , so that they may shirk work, to avoid repetition of duties and functions, so that there may not be any confusion among them to locate responsibility of each and every employee , so that they can complete the whole work in stipulated time, if not then the particular person must be responsible, to establish the sales effort to enforce proper supervision of sales force.

What does the concept of salespeople replacement value mean? What is a sales force turnover management tool? Sales force turnover is defined as the rate at which salespeople leave an organizations, resignations, retirements or dismissals. So, if the organization can raise the sales force turnover ratio, because many salespeople can be promoted or the retirement, or the sales force turnover ratio raising reasons as well as they are not resignation or dismissal reasons. I believe that the organization ought have good sale environment and reasonable reward and welfare strategy to let its salespeople feel happy to help this company to sell its products every day.

However, sales management's actions have direct or indirect effects to impact on turnover. Direct effects may include the firm's firing or dismiss policy. The indirect effects on sale turnover may include new salesperon recruiting and selecting policies affect the quality and performance of the sale force as well as the speed at which salespeople are replaced. The same policies have an impact on the sales force turnover rate through the characteristics of the newly recurited salespersons and the promotion , training, retraining policies, support, supervision, compensation. ALl of those factors have an impact on salesperson's personal satisfaction or dissatisfaction absolutely. So, any sale organizations need to concern how and why whether any one of above these factors may influence their salespeople how to perform or act sale behaviors in order to excite their sale number more effective in long term.

How to achieve sale force management effectively? Sale management is one strategy to many organizations, because organizations expect their salespeople can only raise product sale number. So , they will consider whetther how to implement the sale management strategy to be the most suitable to themselves sale organizations in order to excite their sale teams to sell their products to achieve sale growth aim effectively. So for organization's long term sale growth development, it seems that one excellent sale management strategy can help the organization has stable sale number growth in long term possible.

However, the term " selling" includes a variety of sales situations and activities. For example, those sales positions where the sales representative is required primarily to deliver the product to the customer on a regular or periodic basis. The emphasis is this type of sales activity is very different to the sales position where the sales representative is dealing with sales of capital equipment to industrial purchasers. IN additions some sales representatives deal only in export markets whereas others sell direct to customers in their homes. So, sale organizations need to sell to local or overseas market as well as its target customer is businessmen or individual consumer or both in order to implement to choose their most suitable sale management strategy to train their salespeople more effective or achieving sale growth objective only. Because these its sale major target and where sale market place both factors will influence how it ought train its salespeople, so any organization's training method ought be influenced to change by whom is its major sale target and where is its major sale market location factors.

How to know the psychology of salesmanship? WHen the organization can predict or find reasons to explain why its salespeople feel unhappy to help
this organization to sell its products. Then, it can attempt to improve its weaknesses in order to let its salespeople to feel more sale service satisfactory feeling to continue to help this organization to sell its products. THen, it won't need not often to train or recruit new salespeople to replace its old salespeople in consequence. How to know what its salespeoples' real need in order to raise their sale service satisfactory feeling ?

Psychology means that " science of the mind" and psychology plays to important part in business and it is quite worth to bring to influence any organization salespeoples' posivitive or negative sale emotion in their every sale process between themselves and their every client in personal. For example, if the salesperson often have negative emotion or he feels unhappy in every sale process, then he will encounter or increase many times of sale failure possibilities. He will feel that he is one poor verbal advertiser or seller or promotor to help his organization to promote its products to sell again as well as he will lose confidence to sell any products next sale chance, because his failure sale experiences are accumulated to influence his sale emotion to be poor or difficult sale.

Hence, the poor performance salesperson needs have more successful sale experiences to compensate his / her prior many sale failure times feeling, if the organization hopes this poor performance salesperson can raise sale number easily. Overall, any organizations need to concern how to improve or raise the more failure times of sale experience salespeoples' sale techniques or methods or attitudes more than choose to fire or dismiss them as well as finding another new salesperson to replace him/her. Because it is possible that the salesperson 's poor sale performance that is not due to himself/herself poor sale effort and sale knowledge or lacking sale experience to the product, it may be due to the poor sale team cooperation relationship , feeling poor or not comfortable sale physcial shop environment, poor sale manager and other salespeople working relationship, the sale manager lacks leadership effort, poor family relationship etc. external factors more than himself/herself personal poor or negative emotion or poor health etc. personal factors. Hence, the organization ought enquire him/her why he/she feels unhappy to sell its products and it needs to attempt to find methods to solve his/her challenges immediately. If his/her challenges can be solved. It is possible that his/her sale efforts can be also raised for. So, if the organization can know how to utilize positive sale emotion psychological methods to predict or know why and how every salesperson perform his/her sale behavior in whose daily sale tasks, then it can concentrate on implementing effective and the most suitable sale training to raise their sale abilities more easily.

However, the sale training may include: How to build or improve long term good salesperson and his/her customer sale service relationship between every salesperson and every client in every buying and selling cycle process, how to using right communicating styleds for better understanding every client's real needs, powers and negotiating, e.g. every salesperson needs to review why there are many clients do not choose to buy any products from his sale presentation or promotion, finding every time sale failure reasons can let the salesperson makes himself/herself sale failure reasons evaluation or judgement in order to find what is the major reason influences his/her sale failure, e.g. lacking product knowledge, he/she often let many clients to feel that he lacks patience to listen the client's enquiry or feedback, his sale presentation is not attractive to let many clients like to stay longer time to listen his sale presentation in whole sale process, the salesperson himself/herself emotion is negative and he /she can let many clients feel he / she is not happy or does not enjoy to sell this product from himself/herself face impression or sale behavior impression easily, lacking enough sale techniques to persuade his/her clients why he/she ought choose to buy this product in whole sale process etc. these factors may influence the salesperson's sale failure chance to be raised. Hence sales manager ought need to spend long time to meet the poor sale performance salesperson to discuess what his/her sale challenges are the most major to influence his/her every sale successful chance in order to improve his/ her sale performance more successfully.

IN conclusion, the reasons why salespeople often encounter sale failure possibilities. The factors may include these aspects, such as they lask the desire to help customers to make satisfactory purchase decisons, they only concern how to achieve sale final objective or aim only, it will cause clients feel they do not real concern their real needs. They only concern to sell the product in success. They do not know how to describe the product whether what characteristics or features it owns accurately in order to increase sale chance to persudade them to make final decision to by the product, they do not attempt to participate the whole sale process to help them to choose the most right product in order to satisfy their any purcahse needs, they ought avoid deceptive or manipulative influence tactics, avoid the use of high pressure sales techniques etc. Thus, if any organizations can spend time to investigate what factors cause why any one of salespeople choose perform his/her sale behavior often in order to know or understand their salespeople' sale psychology absolutely. Then, I believe that their sale number will only grown more easily.

● High technological culture change brings what influences to consumer demand change

What does culture level mean? Cultural globalization refers to the transmission of ideas, meanings, and values around the world in

such a way as to extend and
intensify social relations. This process is marked by the common consumption of cultures that have been diffused by the Internet, popular culture media, and international travel. This has added to processes of commodity exchange and colonization which have a longer history of carrying cultural meaning around the globe. The circulation of cultures enables individuals to partake in extended social relations that cross national and regional borders. The creation and expansion of such social relations is not merely observed on a material level. Cultural globalization involves the formation of shared norms and knowledge with which people associate their individual and collective cultural identities. It brings increasing interconnectedness among different populations and cultures.

Nowadays, our culture standard and level trends this direction development, they may include as below:

(1) Diffusion of ideas and cultures amongst all of the civilizations of the world.

(2) Trend that will eventually make all of human experience and customs the same since all cultures are coming together into one.

(3) Occurs in everyday life, through wireless communication, electronic commerce, popular culture, and international trade.

(4) Attempt to promote a Western lifestyle and possibly Americanize the world.

What factors encourage our new cultural development, they may include as below:

(1) New technology and forms of communication around the world help to integrate different cultures into each other.

(2) Transportation technologies and services along with mass migration and individual travel contribute to this form of globalization allowing for cross-cultural exchanges.

(3) Infrastructures and institutionalization embedded change (e.g. teaching languages such as English across the world through educational systems and training of teachers).

The new technological invention cultural influences, I shall indiate these
aspects to explain how they influence
global demand and supply needs increase.

On smart phone product demand aspect,
it seems that new technologic culture can influence the country's any technological products needs in the countries' technological products consumers market. For example, in earlier, smart phones product invention is popular to be accpeted to use in Western countires, e.g. UK, US. So, there are many Western traditional mobile phone Western consumers who change their mobile phones to use smart phones to use. Even, lately, smart phone products are influenced to Asisa countries, e.g. China, Japan, Korea, Singapore etc. these countries traditional mobile phones users also feel smart phones can bring extra non-communication benefits, e.g. internet function. So, technological culture, e.g. internet searching information function , it can influences smart phone demand increases in global mobile market. So, traditional mobile phones can not be accepted to use, because many phones users are influenced to accept to use smart mobile products (it has oral communication and internet functions) by high technological internet communication or gathering or searching any data function culture.

On tansportation technologies and services along with mass migration and individual travel contribute to this form of globalization allowing for cross-cultural exchanges aspect, such as rapid mass transit railway global transportation tools need increase, culture factor has more influential to cause this kind of transport tool needs. For example, Japan and US and UK etc. developed countries have owned rapid mass transit railway transport public tools to let themselves citizens to catch to bring short time journey advantage, such as between homes and working places, or between homes and schools , or between homes and any entertainment places. So, this raid mass transit railway transport culture has influence many developed countries' citizen choose to catch it for their every transport needs in preference, even the developing countries,such as China, Hong Kong have accepted this kind of rapid mass transit railway transport tool culture, they have many passengers also choose to catch this kind of transport tool in preference. So,rapid railway transport tool culture will be global accepted to let any countries' passengers to choose to catch in preference, then , its transport demand will increase in global.

On Infrastructures and institutionalization embedded change (e.g. teaching languages such as English across the world through educational systems and training of teachers)technological culture developement aspect, nowadays, due to internet invention, it raises the distance learning education market development chance, it influence there are many planning overseas learning students, they choose distance learning method to apply internet high technological learning channel to finish any university degrees when they can still to finish their assignments and examinations and send to their overseas universities by email channel. So, this internet high technological invention can bring the distance learning demand increases to global planning overseas learning students choice.

After human improves traditional old culture to new culture, what benefits, it may attribute to business social aspect, they may include:

(1) Allows for profits to companies and nations.

(2) Offers opportunities for development and advancement in economics, technology, and information and usually impacts developed countries.

(3) Creates a more homogeneous world.

(4) Generates interdependent companies amongst companies.

IN fact, human culture development stages, they may include these below several phases as below:

The Pre-modern phase: early civilizations to 1500. It had these characteristics, such as early human migration (facilitation of trade and creation of social networks amongst other nations),emergence of world religions as well as development of trans-regional trade networks (long-distance trade, many centered in China and India. Early forms of globalization, especially with the Silk Road) Then, it enters the modern phase, it had these characteristics, it included medical and industrialization development both aspects, such as european imperialism (rise of the West. European expansionism, especially with Columbus' encounter with the New World which allowed goods and people to cross the Atlantic)

, emerging international economy and international migration and developments outside of the West Spread of modernity Medical advancement that helped many

rise of the nation-state (a development of freedom of movement and cultural diffusion) as well as industrialization development (demand for raw materials to supply industries.

Science grew immensely with electronic shipping, railways, and new forms of communication, such as cable technology).

Finally, it achieves our present contemporary phase: from 1945 to present. It has these characteristics, such as struggle after the cold war led to a slow but steady increase in cultural

flows with the immigration of peoples, ideas, goods, symbols, and images.

Represented global cultural interconnectedness, which eventually led to developments in transport and transport infrastructures such as jet airlines, construction of road and rail networks.

This allowed for more tourism and shifting patterns of global migration. So, nowadays, out culture level development is entering global migration and tourism and high transport technological development phase.

Globalization cultural development or improvement can bring what benefits. I estimate it can bring expanding business chance and economic benefits both aspects as below:

In our business social development benefit aspect, culture improvement can influence these enterprises change to earn more benefits. A visible aspect of the cultural globalization which can create global business market to be expanded to these enterprises, such as American fast food chains. The two most successful global food and beverage outlets, McDonald's and Starbucks, are American companies often cited as examples of globalization, with over 36,000 and 24,000 locations operating worldwide respectively as of 2015.The Big Mac Index is an informal measure of purchasing power parity among world currencies.

In economic benefit aspect, cultural globalization is one of the three main dimensions of globalization commonly found in academic literature, with the two other being economic globalization and political globalization. However, unlike economic and political globalization, cultural globalization has not been the subject of extensive research.

Globalization cultural development or improvement can bring what impacts to our future. It may include these several aspects of impacts. They may include:

The patterns of cultural globalization is a way of spreading theories and ideas from one place to another. Although globalization has affected us economically and politically, it has also affected us socially on a wider scale. With the inequalities issues, such as race, ethnic and class systems, social inequalities plays a part within those categories.

Technology is an impact that created a bridge that diffused the globalization of culture. It brings together globalization, urbanization and migration and how it has affected today's trends. Before urban centers had developed, the idea of globalization after the second world war was that globalization took place due to the lifting of state restrictions by

different nations. There were national boundaries for the flow of goods and services, concepts and ideas.

Hence, global high technological development will influence learning , transport, high tehnological product useful cultures to influence global high technological customers' traditional non-high technological needs to be changed to high technological enjoyment need or demand increase.

● How and why high technological cultural improvement can riase consumption demand

How and why culture is one important factor to influence consumers demand or need change ? Our culture can have different level. In micro economy view, in any organizations, they must have themselves organizational culture. So, their staffs need to follow themselves organizational culture to do any matters. Organizational culture aims to manage or control staff themselves behaviors to avoid they choose to do any wrong or unacceptable decisions to influence team works efficiently. I shall indiate the reasons why any countries need to improve themselve cultures, if they feel their culture is poor as well as how their culture can influence consumer behaviors change, they may include:

(1) Technological development need.

In macro economy view, in any countries, their societies will have themselves unique culture, e.g. US, UK are Western countries, their culture will be open mind more than China, Korea, Japan, Asian countries. IN general, Asian people will have traditional mind, they dislike to accept any new attempts or solve any new challenges.

Otherwise, Western people, such as American, England people who like to accept any new attempts or solve any new challenges. So, it explains that why Western people whose technological development, such sky flight, artificial intelligence etc. and medial development are rapider than any Asia countries. The reason is simple, because they often improve their cutlure to be

better. When they feel that their any technological development is slow and it influences their societies can not earn more benefits or their slow technological development can not attribute any benefits to let themselves countries people live or enjoy more comfortable to compare past. Then, these Western countries will continue to improve their culture level. It aims

to raise their living standard as well as it can satisfy their living needs.

So, culture improvement is important, because it can raise any countries people whose living qualities or standard of living. For example, if the country has many organizations can improve their organizational cultures. Then, they can encourage many staffs have creative effort to invent more new products to attribute to the country's society as well as satisfy their people living needs. So, western countries consumers are influenced to accept to use any new kinds of any products invention more than Asia countries consumers because their cultures are needed to satisfy their living standard and they can to accept any new attempts or solve any new challenges. So, Western consumers,

they are easily to accept to use any kinds of new products more than Asian consumers.

So, when the country has many organizations can improve their cultures and encourage many staffs have creative efforts. Then, any new technological products will be increased to invented in possible. Moreover, themselves people can buy these new technological products to use and they can satisfy their needs and standard of living will also raise. So, when one country has many business firms can improve or change their traditional old culture to develop new creative culture successfully. Then, the country has rapid and successful

organizational cultural improvement to many business firms, they can bring new technological products invention speed to be increase rapidly. Hence, technological development is one reason of cultural improvement. Other reasons may include as below:

(2) Satisfying human's unlimited living needs.

Application of the Maslow's hierarchy of need theory; impacts and implications on organizational culture, human resource and employee's performance Maslow's hierarchy of needs is a theory in psychology anticipated by Abraham Maslow in his 1943 paper "A Theory of Human Motivation". Maslow consequently extended the idea to include his observations of humans' innate curiosity, over the years researches and authors has tend to criticizes the theory as being irrelevant in most part of the world for is western in nature Contrary to such assertion, Maslow's hierarchy of needs theory remains relevant in every sector of our business today as its best analyzes below Maslow's hierarchy of needs where the lower order needs (physiological and safety needs) may be linked to organizational culture. Every new organization passes through this lower order stage in which they struggle with their basic survival needs. At the third level of the Maslow's hierarchy, social needs would correspond to the formation of organized roles within the organization into distinct units, depicting the human resource management function which resonates according to the tone set by organizational culture. The positive interaction of organizational culture and human resource management would result in self-esteem and self-actualization. This is manifested through the employees' performance which showcases the strength and reliability of their organization in the face of competitors. It also implies that the organization through its employees has excelled and met their objectives, mission and vision statement, i.e. a stage that can be considered parallel to self-actualization.

Henece, when any traditional organizational cultures can be continue improved in order to raise their employees performance and efficiency as well as achieve their objectives, mission and vision in short time. Then, they can create more job positions and invent any new technological products to attribute any people to use and raise our living standard.

If the country had many high technological

products organizations have successful organizational culture to encourage employees have good creative effort or abilities to invent any new kinds of high technological products, e.g. the traditional fan products are invented to changed to artificial intelligence fan, which can help any indiviuals to avoide to breaths dirty air and feel cool when they open any (AI) fans in their houses or offices or any working environments or shopping centers etc. public or private internal environment. So, this new (AI) fan product invention will change many traditional fan users to choose (AI) fan in preference. So, if the country has many high technological product sale organizations can encourage their staffs have creative effort to change any traditional old products to new technological products to raise their funtions to bring any consumers advantages. Then, the country will have much new technological products invention to replace traditional old products to be increased demand more easily. So, high technological product creative organizational culture will encourage staffs' creative efforts and it can bring unpredicted any kinds of new high technological products invention chance.

(3) Our societies need to carry on acheive any social progress.

What does social progress mean? Progress is the movement towards a refined, improved, or otherwise desired state.In the context of progressivism, idea of progress refers to the proposition that advancements in technology, science, and social organization have resulted, and by extension will continue to result, in an improved human condition; the latter may happen as a result of direct human action, as in social enterprise or through activism, or as a natural part of sociocultural evolution.

The concept of social progress was introduced in the early 19th-century social theories, especially social evolution as described by Auguste Comte and Herbert Spencer. It was present in the Enlightenment's philosophies of history. As a goal, social progress has been advocated by varying realms of political ideologies with different theories on how it is to be achieved.

How to measure social progress? Specific indicators for measuring progress can range from economic data, technical innovations, change in the political or legal system, and questions bearing on individual life chances, such as life expectancy and risk of disease and disability.

GDP growth has become a key orientation for politics and is often taken as a key figure to evaluate a politician's performance. However, GDP has a number of flaws that make it a bad measure of progress, especially for developed countries. For example, environmental damage is not taken into account nor is the sustainability of economic activity.

Wikiprogress has been set up to share information on evaluating societal progress. It aims to facilitate the exchange of ideas, initiatives and knowledge. HumanProgress.org is another online resource that seeks to compile data on different measures of societal progress.

Our World in Data is a scientific online publication, based at the University of Oxford, that studies how to make progress against large global problems such as poverty, disease, hunger, climate change, war, existential risks, and inequality.The mission of Our World in Data is to present "research and data to make progress against the world's largest problems". For example, on scientific process development aspect,

Scientific progress is the idea that the scientific community learns more over time, which causes a body of scientific knowledge to accumulate.The chemists in the 19th century knew less about chemistry than the chemists in the 20th century, and they in turn knew less than the chemists in the 21st century. Today's chemists reasonably expect that chemists in future centuries will know more than they do. This process differs from non-science fields, such as human languages or history: the people who spoke a now-extinct language, or who lived through a historical time period, can be said to have known different things from the scholars who studied it later, but they cannot be said to know less about their lives than the modern scholars. Some valid knowledge is lost through the passage of time, and other knowledge is gained, with the result that the non-science fields do not make scientific progress towards understanding their subject areas.

From the 18th century through late 20th century, the history of science, especially of the physical and biological sciences, was often presented as a progressive accumulation of knowledge, in which true theories replaced false beliefs. Some more recent historical interpretations, such as those of Thomas Kuhn, tend to portray the history of science in terms of competing paradigms or conceptual systems in a wider matrix of intellectual, cultural, economic and political trends. These interpretations, however, have met with opposition for they also portray the history of science as an incoherent system of incommensurable paradigms, not leading to any scientific progress, but only to the illusion of progress.

Hence, such as Western people have much environment protection needs in their societies, they need to reduce air and water pollution to protect natural environment. For example, environmental damage is not taken into account nor is the sustainability of economic activity. So, environment protection culture can bring environment protection products needs or demands more than Asian people. Also it means that environment protectional culture raises Western manufacturers and Western citizen feel environment protection products needs will increase in Western countries environment protection products market.

● How to develop high technological cultural organizations continue to be improved to raise consumption demand

I shall recommend some solutions to improve cultures to any countries in order to raise consumption demand as below:

(1) In organizational culture improvement aspect, it may include:

Consider the future. The demands of the present often take priority in our work and non-work lives. However, having a vision for the future and long term goals are the starting point for improvement. Start by considering where you see yourself and your company in five to ten years.

· Be honest and specific as you consider where you are now and where you want to be in the future, and determine what you need to do to get from point A to point B.

· For example, if your business has issues with quality control, identify the recurrent issue and map out a plan that resolves it.

· Privilege behavior over production. It's easy to say, "My company will double our profits," but improvements never happen without changing behaviors.

Changing outcomes is a benefit of changing habits, attitudes, and skills.

Write a True North statement.True North statements indicate a change in direction. Consider your business goals and write a few statements that address these goals, and then determine which statement best fits your long term plan. · A True North statement for a business might be "100% customer satisfaction."

Reflect on your past. After deciding on your True North statement, itemize past behaviors that could hinder your overall goal. These behaviors must be modified in order for you to reach your goals. Learn from your past experiences. Continuous improvement comes from reflection, from thinking about situations and really thinking deeply about what went well and what didn't. Think about how you would change things next time, then actually follow through. Also, don't be afraid to try new things."

Start with small improvements, rather than grand, large-scale changes. Think "quality over quantity".

· Small improvements allow you and/or your employees to see results more quickly, which can be a positive reinforcement.

While large improvements are of course the goal, not seeing results for years can foster a sense of disappointment or hopelessness.

· Local improvements can also serve as a model for large scale changes.

Be consistent. Changing everything at once can cause confusion and frustration. Make one change and make sure it sticks before making another change.

· Strive for consistency also as you implement these changes. For instance, if your True North statement was "100% customer satisfaction," one change you might make is to set a standard time span for responses to customer complaints. If you decided that all customer complaints should be answered within six hours, be sure to keep that change consistent.

Starting vision. Employees should understand how they, individually, contribute and are necessary to the larger goals of the company, not just in terms of how what they do benefits an increased profit return, but also how what they do matters in the larger world.

Give clear instructions. Having clear guidelines and clarifying your expectations from the start is important for any collaborative or individual work.

Showing employees how to do something versus telling them how can also clear up any initial questions. · However,demonstrate trust by allowing employees to be in control of their own work. Allow them to determine how they can best complete the task at hand or to make modifications to the changes so that they can complete their work efficiently.

Participate in your vision. Be visible as someone contributing to the goals in everyday ways, rather than simply "overseeing" your employees.

Actions speak louder than words! If your employees see you interacting with customers and responding to customer complaints, you are serving as a model for

future behavior and reminding them through your actions that this goal is important to the overall success of your company.

· Although administrative work is a large part of managing a company, schedule regular intervals to step outside your office and help your employees with their tasks.

· If you run a retail business, for example, help out with stocking inventory, ask customers if you can help them find anything, or work the register.

Allow experimentation.Making room for creative approaches and even failure fosters a positive working environment and allows employees to bring their own talents to the table. · While the goals you have itemized in your plan should be consistent across the board, understand that your employees have different ways of thinking and a variety of skills. One employee's method for resolving a customer complaint, for instance, might not be what you specifically envisioned—it might be even better!

· Consider posing situational examples in group meetings and asking employees how they would resolve the problem. For instance, "X customer has a screaming baby and can't find Y product. How would you help him/her?" Thought experiments can then be tested in the work environment. In the following meeting, have employees reflect on how these experiments went in actuality.

Incentivize employee objectives.While verbal praise offers emotional reward, tangible benefits (such as time or money) also reinforce a job well done and create a positive work environment.

· For example, if your True North statement was "100% customer satisfaction," you might offer a bonus to employees who have had no customer complaints for a month.

· To promote a collaborate environment, you might choose to reward all of your employees with a nice group dinner or a weekend trip if your company meets the quarterly goal.

(2) In social culture improvement aspect, it may include:

IN fact, culture is as a factor of social and economic development. At the present, culture is one of the most impotent factors of development.

The role of culture in development should be treated as multi-layered: on the one hand as an intrinsic value, on secondly as a real factor of regional development

leading to increased attractiveness of regions for tourists, residents and investors, thirdly, as an active factor of social development based on knowledge,

tolerance and creativity. Culture also belongs to a fundamental reference point in relation to metropolitan functions and the significance of cities in spatial,

economic and social arrangements.

Currently observable changes in the economies of highly developed countries demonstrate the increased significance of social capital as a significant factor of economic development, which in large part determines the effective functioning of the economy. Culture, which comprises one of the primary elements of preparation to life in society, plays a particular role in the development of social capital.

Culture related undertakings contribute to an increase in the intellectual potential of regions and the building of a conscious, open and tolerant citizen society. It should be emphasized that culture is a base for initiating cooperation and human communications, performing numerous education functions and thereby activating various layers of society.Culture also comprises a link of social integration, preventing exclusions and social pathologies. At the same time, culture helps to arrange handicapped persons to social and occupational life (e.g. therapy through culture, but largely by changing the mentality and overcoming prejudices).

In general, culture comprises an important factor of social development:

· creates intellectual potential of regions, building human capital,

· through popularization of cultural diversity, creates an aware society, guided by ethical norms, open, resistant to xenophobia,

· prevents social pathologies,

· is a link of social integration,

· is part of national identity,

· preserves local bonds,

· comprises a basis of initiating cooperation and human communication,

· realizes the policy premises of gender equality, racial equality and social solidarity,

· helps restore the mentally and physically handicapped to social and professional life (for example therapy through culture, but especially a change in mentality and overcoming prejudices),

· reduces disproportions of personal development of citizens,

· comprises a form and dimension of social advancement.

How can culture impact economic development? Until recently, culture was perceived as part of social policy and was not tied to economics. This approach changes in the mid 1990s. Since that time, a growing impact of culture on the economy is observable – three different trends are spoken of:

The "economisation of culture", "commodification of culture" and the "culturalisation" of the economy.

This is accompanied by a huge increase in the number of academic papers and programmes concerning the subject of the economy and employment in the field of culture.

Investments undertaken in the field of culture – besides intangible, social profits – frequently have an economic dimension as well. The subsidy amount for cultural undertakings is multiplied, owing to culture industries, which contribute to increased employment and generate gross national product value. It should be pointed out that investments in cultural infrastructure fulfil, just as other public expenditures, functions of development multipliers.

There are two kinds of cultural imnpact to investment effects. Two effects of investments undertaken in the field of culture can be distinguished as below :

One of them is the expansion of the regional economic base that comprises an impulse for further development. This development is expressed by improvement

of the market and marketing situation of existing commercial entities (e.g. a positive change in a region's image), improvement in the standard of living of residents (expansion of the cultural infrastructure and increased access to culture) as well as an increase in the number of jobs associated with the investment realization process,

and then with the functioning of new elements of a region's fixed assets.

The second effect results from the stimulating impact of public expenditures by income – demand multipliers. Increasing the income of commercial entities and households, these expenditures stimulated additional demand, which has a large impact on local markets for goods and services.

Why do culture industries also have a significant share in the economic development of societies and regions?

One of the most common definitions of the notion of a "culture industry" relates to all private businesses and independent contractors active in publishing, artistic,

music, film or audiovisual industries. This definition can be expanded to other related products and services, for example to cultural tourism or the media.

Besides the subject of action on affiliation to culture industries, earnings related criteria are decisive. The size of entities does not play a role here;

they can be individual artists, small and mid-sized enterprises or large media concerns.

Culture industries are characterised by a high level of innovation and creativity in the market, where most goods and services cannot be properly substituted.

Culture industries create jobs outside the public sector. Various culture industry sectors in which mid-sized and small enterprises dominate, have large employment potential and are strongly anchored in local communities and regional networks. Cultural industries are the sector of the economy with the highest employment factor. They generate a large number of jobs, in an age of cooling off or even stagnation of the world economy. The sector of culture industries is today, after undergoing difficulties caused by over-investment in

the dotcom and computer-network sector – the most dynamically growing branch of the world economy. It creates strong economic incentives due to the high level of final product transformation.

Thus, it requires a highly qualified workforce, professionals of specific specializations, employing university graduates of various majors, creating developmental conditions of

society educated at a high intellectual potential.For example, Asian and Western people eating culture is different, Asian like to drink tea,cook rice. Otherwise, Western like to drink milk,soft drink, eat potato replaces rice. So, Asian countries' rice and tea food demand must be more than Western as well as Western countries' pototo and soft drink food demand must be more than Asian. Hence, food culture will influence the countries' different kinds of food demand number.

● Lacking high technological cultural organizational improvement disadvantages influence to consumption market

What are the disadvantages, when one country or organization had not improved itself country culture as well as how their poor cultures can influence themselves countries' consumption market in long time? I believe that they may include as below:

On organizational lacking culture improvement aspect, one lacking culture improvement organization, it may have these disadvantages to decrease its consumer number consequence, Disadvantages of Continuous Improvement may include below, such as

.Inefficiency. A continuously lacking improving business is continually improving inefficiency. As you can not implement the systems to get more done in less time, you save less money on labor and decrease customer satisfaction by turning out a higher-quality product.

· less engagement. Employees who work in an poor working environment where they are not expected to make continual improvements and they are not more interested in their work than employees who are expected to simply show up and get the job done. Interested employees are satisfied employees who stay with your company longer and satisfy customers and fix problems.

· less customer satisfaction. As your products and services can not continually improve, you'll not be better able to meet customer needs. Your offerings will decrease because your staff will not be

devoting time and energy toward resolving difficulties. These efforts will not be in part a response to customer feedback,
and their implementation will not improve the customer experience.

· ineffective systems. When lacking continuous improvement is part of a poor quality management effort, your business will not put systems in place to continually evaluate and upgrade its operations. These systems will not give your company the tools it needs to build quality into its DNA as an intrinsic aspect of its identity.

Advantages of continuous improvement may include below, such as:

.There isn't any real downside to improvement itself unless your business model is based on coasting by with a substandard or merely adequate product.
However, some of the systematic protocols and approaches to achieving continuous improvement may not always work in the best interest of your business.

· Incremental improvement. Continuous improvement is usually implemented as an incremental process in which advances are made in small steps according to an
established set of assumptions. To have a formal continuous improvement program in place, your team will have defined a set of desirable objectives and will be working
toward these outcomes. However, sometimes real improvement comes from shattering a mold and exploring an entirely different direction.

· exciting innovation. If your business has defined the ways it wants to grow and improve, it may limit itself to a specific type of development and close
itself off to other possibilities. It addition to missing opportunities, this creates the possibility of stifling rather than rewarding the creativity of your staff.

· Inadequate implementation. Although continual improvement itself tends to be good for an organization, it may not be implemented effectively. Objectives may not be communicated clearly, or managers may not be sufficiently motivated in following through with improvements. If your staff

isn't sufficiently motivated or if they feel like their efforts are wasted, your continuous improvement program may create more problems than benefits.

On social lacking culture improvement aspect, the country's society may bring these disadvantages to discourage the country itself consumption environment such as below:

On social culture diversity disadvantages aspect, in many ways, diversity is a major advantage to an industrialized society. Diversity provides

labor resources and cultural vitality to first world countries that would otherwise be severely impacted by aging populations. However, this does not mean that diversity

comes without difficulties. Among the most noticeable disadvantages of cultural diversity include language barriers, social tension, and civic disengagement.

It should be noted that these are not reasons to avoid diversity, but rather, factors to keep in mind as society heads toward a more diverse future.

The country's cultural diversity may bring these negative influences to its society. They may include:

(1) Language Barriers

One of the main disadvantages of cultural diversity is its tendency to create language barriers. Social segregation often occurs when speakers

of two mutually unintelligible languages live side by side. Language barriers are generally temporary in nature (most immigrants eventually learn the language

of the country they move to), but the resultant segregation can endure, as exemplified in segregated neighborhoods and ethnic ghettos. As a result of this phenomenon,

many governments around the world now require that prospective immigrants learn their country's official language.

(2) Social Tension

Social tension can occur as a result of cultural and linguistic differences. In Europe, for instance, tension between the Muslim minority and the

largely secular majority is frequently attributed to the incommensurability of Islamic and Secular values. The tensions caused by culture are thought to be

exacerbated by economic differences, as European Muslim populations are frequently disadvantaged in employment due to a lack of educational opportunities. According

to Harvard professor Robert B. Putnam, these kinds of tensions often result in populations "hunkering down" in their homes instead of interacting with their neighbors.

(3) Civic Disengagement

Civic disengagement is not a consequence one would expect from social diversity. However, studies have shown that civic disengagement is more

likely to occur in diverse communities than in relatively homogeneous communities. According to an aggregate study by Matthew Kahn and Dora Costa, when cultural

diversity is combined with income inequality, members of all cultural and income groups are less likely to volunteer or become politically involved. This effect

is most likely to be observed when an immigrants are systematically placed at an economic disadvantage, whether due to immigration policy or workplace discrimination.

(4) Workplace Issues

Occasionally, workplace issues can arise from cultural diversity. White employees sometimes feel institutionally discriminated against in diverse workplaces, perceiving diversity instruments (e.g., the disparate impact test) to be a form of reverse discrimination. Conversely, African-American employees often feel socially discriminated against in diverse workplaces, especially when the workplace has an all-white management team. According to one study, African American employees are 2.5 times as likely to resign from a job at a diverse workplace than a white employee is, while a female employee is twice as likely to leave a diverse workplace than a male employee is. These numbers add some statistical weight to reports of discrimination and exclusion directed toward minority and female

employees at diverse workplaces.

All of above issues which will be the poor effects when one country has more cultural diversity or difference in itself society. So, one high cultural

diversity country will have let its people to feel comfortable to live and workers will feel difficulties to adapt to work in their working environment or working

places, because they have sex, age or Asian/Western skin discrimination between them. Then, they must not feel happy to work when they are working together in

their high discrimination workplaces. Even, students will feel difficulties to adapt to learn in their schools, for Asian students overseas learning case example, when the classroom has less Asia students and

many Western students. The Western students must discrimine the Asia students in the school's classroom. When these Asia students need to contact these Western students, but they perform their attitudes and behaviors are not kindly to them, so these Asian student must feel not polite from these Western students. Finally, these Asian students' learning performance or examination results will be influenced to be poor by their poor treatment or poor contact. So, poor culture or lacking culture improvement to the country, it will cause unhappy working environment or learning environment in the country's any schools or workplaces in common.

On conclusion, when any countries are lacking culture improvement to themselves any business organizations or societies that will bring disadvantages to reduce or disencourage the consumption chance in themselves societies, so if any countries hope themselves societies' technology and living of quality can be improved to satisfy their people's living needs. They must not neglect how to improve themselves cultures to be better to let their people to feel when they are living in themselves countries.

CHAPTER III

Long Time Working Hours Bring Negative Influence

Hong Kong labors abnormal long time working hours organizational culture

This research is about Hong Kong employers need labors to work abnormal long time working hours whether it can assist Hong Kong economic growth and raise productivity both in the long term.

The outcome is either Hong Kong labors work long time working hours abnormally who can not rise Hong Kong economic growth or who can rise Hong Kong economic growth in long time. Generally, Hong Kong employers choose to pay less salary expenditure to need many extra labors to work abnormal working hours to help them to rise productivity, but who don't concern that long time working factor will influence unhealthy to current workers due to who need to work long time working hours abnormally in long time and it seems to cause their workers will reduce productivity and inefficiency in long time.

Although, it is possible that HK labors can be increased extra abnormal working hours to work to rise Hong Kong employers' productivity and assist HK social economy will be grown up in short term, but it is also possible that it can't rise Hong Kong economic growth due to their unhealthy or sick increasing to cause productivity declining and inefficiency in long time. Thus, I shall find evidence to analyze whether Hong kong labors need to work abnormal long time working hours. Otherwise, who will decline Hong Kong economic growth and reduce productivity and inefficiency in long time as well as I shall give suggestion to indicate whether either current workers work abnormal long time working hours or employers ought choose to employ more extra part time workers to assist current labors to rise their productivity to decide which is the best choice to raise HK economic growth and efficient productivity in long time.

1.1 What is abnormal working hours Economic Problem

Effects on Hong Kong employment of working time reduction is found to be difficult to predict. The results of Hong Kong macroeconomic simulations of the effects on employments of working time reduction rely heavily on certain basic assumptions, such as how many hours people will actually work or how productivity and pay levels will develop. Whether HK abnormal working hours will assist HK social economic growth or economic falling down in long term.

The reasons cause Hong Kong labours who need to work abnormal long time working hours. In fact, it isn't the reason that the Hong Kong high skilful labours market is shortage to supply for the nature of some occupations, e.g. hospital doctors and nurses, university teachers, law firm lawyers etc professional occupations. Hk has many high qualification university students graduation, it has enough labor supply to high labor market evey year. The reason is that employers don't like to spend more salary to increase to employ extra labors to share current workers workload, such as low skilful and hardworking labors, such as cleaners, securities, waiters and high skilful professionals, such as hospital doctors and nurses, university teachers, lawyers etc. However, the low and high skilful labor market can be enough supply in Hong Kong, but Hong Kong employers need the current high and low both skilful workers who need to work more than 10 to 12 hours or more per working day commonly. It is possible that HK high and low educational labours will be caused unhealthy and lack enough sleep if who still need to work abnormal working hours time in long time. Although, who can rise productivity and efficiency in the short time, but it is possible that who can't rise productivity and inefficiency in the long time. Moreover, it will cause many young or middle or old ages high educational or low educational knowledgeable hardworking workers who will lose many jobs provided and who will be hard to find any jobs in HK labor employment market if HK employers don't choose to pay extra salaries to employ extra full time workers to share current labors' workload in the high and low salary occupations, due to they only choose to increase abnormal additional extra working hours to current workers to achieve to reduce employment expenditure and raise productivity. Hence, it is possible to influence HK social economy grows up slowly, even it's economy can go down seriously in long time.

● Hypotheses Testing And Data Analysis

I shall assume that working wage or salary of every individual labors can not be increased, even can be decreased as well as whose normal working hours can be increased abnormally in generally. This means that the Hong Kong individual worker's income will be decreased and general productivity raising is not affected generally, due to HK employers need current labors to work abnormal extra working hours to attempt to raise productivity daily, but their salary or wage have not increased more. However, HK employers need many workers to accomplish the same amount of work, even who don't like to employ extra labors to assist current workers to achieve long term productivity rasing in their companies. These abnormal working hours labors will feel unfair treatment, due to they need to work abnormal working hours, but their salary or wage have not been increased.

In the first scenario of my hypothesis is about that HK labor employment market's general salary or wage has not been increased to the normal proportion of the increased extra abnomal working time(hours). Then, in HK labors market, due to the numbers of labors supply is more than the jobs supply because HK employers don't like to pay more salary or wage expenditure to employ extra labor, but they like to increase extra abnormal working hours to current workers to aim to achieve productivity. So it will cause many HK job seekers with adequate qualifications or with less qualifications who won't find any jobs easily, then the HK the numbers of unemployed people will be increased and their household incomes will decrease to cause many HK household do not like to spend easily. The result will cause a negative effect on HK social private consumption will be decreased and the businessmen' income will be decreased also. So, HK people private consumption decreasing will influence HK economy growth to be slow, even it will cause HK economy declining in the long time.

In the second scenario of my hypothesis is about that Hong Kong workers are fully compensated for the increasing extra abnormal working time(hours) by the abnormal additional working hours calculation. Although, Hong Kong companies' productivity will be raised, but which are not to the extent that it compensates Hong Kong enterprises for their increased wage or salary costs. In fact, Hong Kong enterprises, their costs are passed on to the clients, it causes Hong Kong's economic growth has an impact on international competitiveness to cause economic declining in possible when these enterprises need to raise their products' sale prices to balance their salary or wage cost rasing to win their import competitors. Another effect is that Hong Kong individual labor's incomes decrease, which means that Hong Kong private consumption also falls in this scenario to influence HK economic growth seriously. Thus, the HK economic growth problem will be caused, due to these factors lead to a fall in Hong Kong social household private consumption. Consequently, it will cause many HK employers hope to raise Hong Kong productivity and they will raise the total amount of Hong Kong labor actually worked hours will be risen to such as extent as the increasing in normal working time(hours) from 8 or 9 hours per normal working day to 10 or 11 or 12 hours, even more extra abnormal hours per working day to the current labors. But they do not like to spend more salary or wage expenditure to employ full time extra labors, instead of increasing extra abnormal working hours to current labors to achieve productivity of raising, due to the cost will be increased if they choose to employ extra full time labors if they want to raise productivity. However, I feel they will raise productivity in the short term, but they will not raise productivity in the long term when they choose to raise their current labors abnormal working hours per working day.

The assumption will be made regarding to the relationship between the HK labor market's abnormal long time working hours factor and whether it can influence Hong Kong economic growth in long time for this research economic problem. For example, how many hours Hong Kong labor would actually work or how much workers have efficient productivity and efficiency and how much salaries or wages would be affected as a result of the increasing in working time(hours) in Hong Kong employment market.

I shall apply endogenous growth theory to Hong Kong labor market. As this theory indicates that this model also incorporated a new concept of human capital, whose capital is increasing rates of return. Research done in this area has focused on what increases human capital (e.g. education) or technological change (e.g. innovation) to influence HK economic growth. In macro economic environment, it indicates that economic growth means the increase in the market value of the products and services produced by the country's economy over time. It is conventionally measured as the percent rate of increase in real growth domestic product or real GDP. The growth of the ratio of GDP to population (GDP per capital, per capita income). Thus, an increase in growth is caused by more efficient use of inputs is referred to as intensive growth. GDP growth is caused only be increased in such as capital, population or territory is called extensive growth. Thus, in economy growth theory, typically refers growth off potential output, i.e. production is at full employment. However, HK unemployment ratio is still high to compare other developed or developing countries, although the labors supply are enough to HK employment market.

The working time is the period of time that an individual spends at paid occupation labor. Many countries regulate the work week by law, such as minimum daily rest periods, annual holidays and a maximum number of working hours per week. Working time may vary from person to person often depending on location, cultural, lifestyle choice and the profitability of the individual's livelihood.

Generally, most Hong Kong employers need labours work long time working hours abnormally. For example, low educational workers, such as security occupations of labors need to work per working day is twelve hours or more, restaurant waiters and dish cleaners also need to work ten to twelve hours or more per working day, bank counter cashiers or audit firm staffs also need to work over time from 10 to 12 hours or more per working day and who have no extra salaries for over time salaries payment commonly. Standard working hours or normal working hours refers to the legislation to limit the working hours per day, per week, per month or per year. If an employee needs to work overtime, the employer will need to pay overtime payments to employees as required in the law. Generally speaking, standard working hours countries wordwide are around 40 to 44 hours per week (but not everywhere: such as France employers need labors work from 35 hours per week, North Korea employers need labors work up to 112 hours per week). Maximum working hours refers that the employee can't work than the level specified in the maximum working hours law. It seems that Hong Kong many employers had needed labors to work above standard working hours per week to compare to other developed countries, e.g. America, France, England, New Zealand etc. developed countries.

On the 20th century, work hours are declined by almost half, mostly due to rising wages are brought about by renewed economic growth with a supporting role from legislation human rights. The decline countined at a faster in Europe: For example, France adopted a 35 hours work week in 2000 year. In 1995, China adopted a 40 hours week, eliminating half day work on Saturday. Technology has also continued to improve worker productivity, permitting standards of living to rise as hours declined. In developed economies, as the time needed to manufacturing products has declined more working hours have become available to provide services. In fact, on the one hand, Hong Kong manufacturing industry has declined, such as clothing, shoes, toy etc. manufacturing industry. On the other hand, its service industry need many labors to supply in the labor market per day, e.g. banking, accounting, restaurant, security etc. service sectors. A reduction in Hong Kong working time can be accomplished in various ways, and that Hong Kong enterprise's production costs will be affected in different ways depending on what type of measured is used. Usually Hong Kong employers would be likely to ask those already employed to do more overtime or who will require part time workers to increase whose working hours, especially would pass salaries expense from them on to charge higher sale price to their clients. Then, which would increase the rate of inflation and weaken competitiveness to win overseas competitors' product import.

I shall use these methods to examine this research problem, e.g. statistical analysis and economic concepts, such as GDP, economic growth and labor participation rate. Aim to research whether HK abnormal long time working hours can raise productivity and influence HK economic growth in long term. As regards Hong Kong enterprises' productivity, my research will be discussed what factors that may lead to either an increase or a decrease in productivity and I shall conclude what the effects are very difficult to assess as conditions vary between and it will concern within different service industry sectors, e.g. hotel, bank, restaurant, security, professional service etc. service occupations. These service labors of numbers are more than manufacture labors of numbers in Hong Kong nowadays. Of vital importance for the effect on Hong Kong employment of a reduction of working time is the extent to which wages or salaries are adopted. If the occupations where there was a shortage of labors, Hong Kong employers were to try to contibute to higher pay claims to long time working labors. According to the 1961 year population census, the size of the economically active population was approximately 1.2 million during that year and who was also economically active population was seeking worker. The labor force had grown to 3.1 million by 1996 year (William. C & Wing. S, 1997).

In 1996 year, HK economy was industrialization process filled by a large supply of relativey unskilled but hardworking labor, many of them were refugees from China, the dominance of manufacturing has been largely displaced by commerce and service sector and the demand for unskilled labor is falling relative to the demand for skilled and educated workers in Hong Kong. According to the 1961 year population census, the size of the economically active population was approximately 1.2 million during that year and who was also economically active population or the active seeking worker. The labor force had grown to 3.1 million by 1996 year (William. C & Wing. S, 1997). William. C & Wing. S (1997) also indicated that HK Census and Statistics department (various years) reported specific labor participation rate and size of the Hong Kong force from 1961 year to 1996 year. "During this period the size of the labor force grew from 1.2 million to 2.5 million. The annual rate of increase was 3.7%. It implies labor supply increased so rapidly, so labor intensive industries were developed. However, Hong kong population had increased to 7 million till to 2015 year." Hence the size of the labor force had increased more and it implied labors would supply more than employers demand. But, HK employer job supply numbers are less than HK labor demand numbers in HK employment market. It seems that if HK employers did not like to spend more salaries expenditure to employ extra labors to rise productivity, it would cause many young single or married people unemployed.

Any countrie's economic growth are usually calculated in real terms. i.e. inflation adjusted terms to eliminate the effect of inflation on the price of products produced. Economic growth has the indirect potential to reduce poverty, as a result of an increase in employment opportunities and increased labor productivity. However, employment is no guarantee of escaping poverty. The international labor organization estimates that is as many as 40% of workers are poor, not earning enough to keep families above the $2 a day poverty line. For instance, in India, poor are wage earner in formal employment because jobs are insecure and low paid and offer no chance to accumulate wealth to avoid risk, other countries found bigger benefits from focusing more no productivity improvement than low skilled work. Thus, increase in employment without increase in productivity lead to rise in the number of working poor and these countries don't apply the creation of quality and not quantity in labor market policies. In Vietnam, for example, employment growth has slowed when productivity growth has continued. Furthermore, productivity increases don't always lead to increase wages, e.g. United States, the gap between productivity and wages was been rising since the 1980 year. The overseas Development Institute study showed that other sectors were just as important in reducing unemployment as manufacturing.

Nowadays, the services sector is most effective as translating productivity growth into employment growth in Hong Kong. The HK Government forecast (2012) indicated that "HK's economy has slowed, growing by 0.9% year-on year in the half of 2012 year, after expanding by 5% in 2011 year. For 2012 year, the economy is forecast to grow at 1-2%. Consumer prices increased by 5.3% in 2011 year and 4.7% year-on-year in the first half of 2012 year. The unemployment rate was 3.2% for April-June 2012 year, compared with 3.4% for 2011 year." Although, it seemed that unemployment rate decreased 0.2% for April to June 2012, but its unemployment was still existed. Moreover, HK's economy has slowed to grow by 0.9% only year-on-year in the first half of 2012 year and HK government forcast to grow at 1-2% for 2012. By United States Government statistic in 2006 year, the average man employed full time worked 8.4 hours mandatory minimum amount of paid time off for sickness or holiday. However, regular full time workers often have the opportunity to take about nine days off for various holiday. However, regular full time workers of skill leave and two weeks (10 business days) of paid holiday time with some workers receiving additional time after several years. Because of the pressure of working time with some workers receiving additional time after several years. It seems United States developed countries some workers still feel pressure of working shorten working hours can reduce the pressure of working. In fact, HK many professional workers put in longer hours than the forty hour standard per week. A forty hours work week is considered inadequate and may result in job loss or failure to be promoted. Although, these employers don't spend much salary expenditures to employ extra professional workers to share whose workload and who can perform to serve whose clients efficiently in the short time. But in the long time, it is possible that who will work pressure possibly due to who need to serve many clients every day, and whose working performance will become to be poor to cause inefficiently. Until now, HK has no legislations regarding maximum and normal working hours. The average weekly working hours of full time employees in HK is 49 hours. According to the Price and Earnings report (2012) conducted by UBS, when the global and regional average were 1,915 and 2,154 hours per year respectively, the average working hours in HK is 2,296 hours per year, which ranked the fifth longest yearly working hours among 72 countries under study. In addition, the survey is conducted by the public opinion study group of the University of HK, it showed 79% of the respondents agree that the problem of overtime work in HK is "serve" and 65% of the respondents agree that the legislation on the maximum working hours. In HK, 70% of surveyed don't receive any overtime remuneration. These show that people in HK concerns the working time issues. The equilibrium price for a certain types of labor is the wage rate. The model of labor market, even given all its assumption is logically. The criticism of application of the model of supply and demand generalizes particularly to all markets for factor of production, e.g. labor working hours. I assume HK employers don't like to employ many labors to assist current labors to raise service or productivity when their client numbers have increased. It is possible that who feel salaries expenditure can not be exceed to their reasonable budget. Hence, who need current labors to work long time hours to do too much work, even the HK labor supply is increasing and it will cause many people lose jobs. It seems HK service industry can influence its economic growth. If those service industry labors need to work long time, who will feel mental pressure to work unhealthly and who need have enough sleep. If who can't have enough sleep to face every day work in long term, whose working performance will be poor or reduce productivity to whose clients possibly in long time. I believe HK service industry labors work long time working hours per week that it will influence whose service performance to be poor. In fact, most developed countries labors working hours are less than HK seriously. For example, United States originating from the traditional American business hours of 9:00 AM to 5:00 PM. Monday to Friday, representing a workweek of five to eight hour per working day composing 40 hours in total. The actual time at work often varies between 35 and 48 hours in practice due to breakers. In many traditonal white collar positions, employees were required to be in the office during these hours to take orders from the bosses, workplace hours have become more flexible. Another example, South Korea has the fastest declining working time, which is the result of proactive more to lower working hours at all levels to increase leisure and than the 10 days of the united States and double that of the England's 8 days. Also, work hours in and 40 hour week (44 hours in specified workplaces). The overtime limits are: 15 hours a week, allowance should not be lower than 125% and not more than 150% of normal hourly rate. However, Hong Kong dish cleaners, bank cashiers occupations whose need to work over time often , due to client numbers are increasing every days and their employers do not plan to employ extra workers to share their work loading. Hence, it seems whose work over time are similar to work abnormal long time working hours in every week in HK.

Middison A.(2001) indicated that "the unemployment rate is a performance indicator of the economy." The purpose of economic activity is to transform productive resources into products and services. An economy that uses all or most of its labor force should clearly be considered as a better performing economy than one that lacks the ability to put all or most of its labor force into work and thus some labor productive respurces can not be used. In fact, in economy theory, labor demand is considered to be a derived demand, meaning that its demand is explained not by itself, but by the existence of demand for products and services that use labor as a factor production. If labor demand is a desired demand, then an assessment of the performance of the economy could certainly profit from an evaluation of how well a specific social system managers to transform labor input into products and services. It is convenient to distinguish between economic performance of an economic system and labor market performance. The former related with the ability of a social system to deliver products and services and the latter related with the important, but more specific issue, of how well the labor market managers to match supply and demand. Economic and Trade Information on HK (2012) key indicators of the labor market had finished sample simple average of 15 countries statistic analysis to show "the result was as for the role of work hours in explaining GDP per capital had negative relation between GDP and working hours, as if long working hours where used to compensate the low productivity. The historical downward trend of working time form the slightly less than 3000 annual hours per person employed of the 1870 year to the less than 1600 year of the late 1990 year could be taken as a confirmation of this hypothesis." Thus, this hypothesis could be supported by viewpoint. It was about HK long time working hours ought not increase HK GDP and long working hours where used to compensate the low productivity to HK employers in the long time.

● What is the difference of benefits between normal working hours and abnomral working hours organizational culture

These research will have these two questions to be answer:

1. Can Hong Kong this individual labour abnormal long time working hours factor gives welfare benefit to every labor in the long time?

2. Can Hong Kong this abnormal labor working hours factor grow HK society whole economy in the long time?

It seems that HK employers don't like to employ extra workers to share current worker's workload, even the supply of labours is enough. Due to who do not want to pay extra each worker's salaries to raise whose productivity. To explain relationship between the workers abnormal long time working hours factor and the other resources input factor to influence HK enterprises growth in an improved model in the long time. I shall develop a model is the selection of two variables to explore. These variables have a cause and effect relationship. I shall suppose HK employers believe that workers abnormal long time working hours which can raise their productivity efficiently and which can assist HK society overall economic growth in the long time. These variables have a cause and effect relationship. From this discussion to investigate HK society overall economic growth effect is caused by companies' variable factors. The variable factors include the raising of abnormal long time working hours factor or increasing capital and machinery and equipment and building assets factor or raising natural resources for production factor or taking risking of success or failure ability in an productive enterprise factor. Thus, these separate sets of variable have been indentifies and each set could be selected for a model. In fact, Hong Kong society overall economic growth disputes many occur because a variety of resources input factors can be considered to analyze an effect cause whether which kind of resources input factors which can cause HK society economy growth is fast or slow. In my viewpoint, my exploring reasons are for a slow growing economy in HK. Some economists focus on relationship between money supply and growth in society, some in society's spending growth and some on the price level. In fact, HK economic growth is slow in the long time. I shall focus on the relationship between the HK companies' workers abnormal long time working hours factor and the other resources input factor both to influence HK society overall economic growth. Hence, I shall give assupmtions and conditions are held to be true when exploring the relationship is between HK companies and resources input variables within a model. For example, the relationship is between HK economic growth is slow or fast and labor resources supply numbers are not shortage. But HK employers ususally employ their limited numbers of labors to cause current workers need to overtime work or work in abnormal long time working hours often. Understanding the factors behind labor participation decision is an important component of the understanding long time change in labor supply in Hong Kong society.

In my another viewpoint, discussing HK labor supply, it is important to distinguish between the supply economy. The supply of Hong Kong labor to particular firm, an industry can be highly responsive to wages or salaries as workers seek the most profitable employment in HK. The supply of labors to HK society economy. On the other hand, it is typically less elastic to the labors who often change new jobs because most HK employers who need workers who work long time working hours to cause most HK labors can't have much chance to change new jobs which can provide normal working hours. So, it seems that who won't choose to change new jobs often because many HK employers who need HK labors work abnormal working hours nowadays.

HK employees of large companies of public utilities sector and the HK Government both organizations which typically enjoy more benefits and have greater job security than employers of small firms in Hong Kong society. This has lead to cause a distinction between the small HK private companies and public HK Government and public utilities sector. In fact, nowadays, most HK jobs have changes to service job nature from manufacturing job nature. However, deregulation, downsizing and pressure factors have caused many HK large companies which choose change working hours from normal 7 to 8 hours per working day to adnormal 9 to 12 hours or more per working day. Specically, the occupations of service sector job nature include: restaurant waitors, banking counter servicers, professional lawyers, share agents, security servicers, accountants etc. different service sector occupation labors. The result will cause the labors who choose to leave whose employers if who could not accept to work abnormal working hours to their current employers. Even, it will also cause the current workers who feel nervous and tired and worry to work in pressure everyday, due to who need to increase many extra hours to work often and who will lose their private entertainment time with their family or friends often, even it will be unhealthy to them due to who lack sleeping. Although, HK business cycle was the short term economy in manufacturing macroeconomic environment in beginning from 1950 year. Then, HK economy growth had developed, so many the demanding of labor numbers had been caused to increase seriously till to nowadays. The economic and trade information on Hong Kong of HK Government statistic department (2012) reported " the HK economy was forecasted to grow at 1-2% for 2012 year and it's economy had slowed growing by 0.9% per year in the half of 2012 year after expanding by 5% in 2011 year." Although, it implied that HK labor market had enough labor numbers supply. Otherwise, many HK employers don't like to employ many labor numbers to share current workers' workload. It is possible that due to whose HK current workers need to spend adnormal working hours to raise their productivity per working day to save spending extra salaries or wages expenditures to pay to employ extra labors in HK current labor market. I feel that HK economy growth is slow or poor because the main reason is due to HK Government doesn't spend expenditures to assist HK employers to raise training to their current HK labors to provide human capital to achieve to raise whose service performance to improve their efficient productivity in HK service businesses sector only in the long time. Finally, the results were discovered and will be backed by these evidences.

- abnormal working hours cultural influences
-

My essay will truly be a qualitative and quantitative research, it is based on experimental fact and evidence. To research the long time employment influence relationship is between the labor abnormal long time working hours factor and the influence of HK economic growth in productive model factor both. This study suggests understanding of the relationship between economic growth influences and HK labors abnormal working hours need to be raised. In fact, the HK labor force participation rate will be fallen every year. Economic growth in HK was through phases that affects growth through changes in the labor force participation rate and the relative sizes of HK society service and manufacturing sectors. In fact, HK agricultural industry sector is not existed and manufacturing industry sector numbers are decreasing and it begins to enter service industry sector. The low knowledge level of jobs include security, banking, restaurant, cleaning, transportation etc. service nature of jobs as well as the high knowledge level of jobs include lawyer, accountant, medicine, doctor, computer technician etc. professonal service nature of jobs which both are providing service to HK society nowadays. The investment theory indicates that the education is as investment human capital to provide to any companies. The main difference is that human capital is incorporated in human beings and it can't be resold. When physical capital can be acquired at almost any desired amount in boom periods and be resold during recession on secondary markets, human capital can be acquired mostly in the beginning of individual behavior by firms. I shall recommend HK companies ought choose these methods to control labors whose working hours time efficiently.

Yasuhiro (2014) showed that "wage differentials based on age and length of service in-house training refers to a process whereby workers acquire skills through daily work and occasional of the job training. Whether or not they perceive it as "training" is irrelevant. Training is also included informal learning conducted independently by the worker without any feedback from an instructor. Conceptually, the skills acquired are divided into general skills that can be used in the company currently employing the worker. The process of acquiring the latter specific training." Generally, when companies minimizes personnel costs, the ratio of marginal productivity referred to below as productivity between workers are equal to wage ratios. Therefore, the coefficient of age in the wage function expresses the rate of productivity increases due to general training and the coefficient of length of service and the rate of wage increases due to special training reason. The sum of both coefficients will express the rate of productivity increase in current companies due to training is as an important causing factor. In conclusion, in my viewpoint, HK employers need to provide on job training to current labors to aim to raise their efficiency to productivity in the long time. Because when their labors had been trained to let them to learn how to use special skill to finish their job duties easily, then they will not need to spend much time (additional working hours) to finish their job duties per working day. On the one hand, HK employers need to measure to compare what benefits are in favour of standard working hours to whose employees. The benefits include, such as promoting work life balance and enjoy family life, increasing time for leisure and rest, beneficial to health and employees can have more time to pursue further studies as well as employers do not need to pay higher salaries to longer working hours employees or overtime pay boost income as most HK companies pay time and a half to some employees only. On the other hand, HK employers need to measure to compare what benefits are against standard working hours to employers, such as employing many part time working hours employees to assist normal working hours full time employees rather than needing full time employees work abnormal hours daily, lowering or cancelling year and bonues etc. Moreover, HK employers may also use various measure to offset the increased cost of running businesses, such as lowering average hourly anual compensation. However, when HK employees are forced to work part time jobs, who may need to acquire additional employment to maintain their standard living. Even, HK employers only force employees to work overtime in some situations. Appropriate standard working hours can vary across different industries based on the type of work performed. Such as some HK certain professional positions are difficult to define in terms of appropriate working hours. Issues can arise with employers expecting exployees to work extra hours "off the clock" in order to keep costs down. Thus, I believe that HK labors abnormal working hours time issue ought be decreased and HK employers ought employ extra workers assistance to share current labors' workload to help them to raise productivity and efficiency and HK economy will grow fast in the long time. Finally, my research aims to find that the number of hours worked is a more responsive measure of the state of the labor market than employment in HK. Comparing the number of hours worked to indicators of the wider economy shows that it is likely to be demand from HK firms (employers) which is driving the numbers of hours, rather than individual job applicant supplys to HK employment market. My analysis also show that the HK appears to have developed a long working hours culture to compare other developed countries, such as America, England, Canada etc. In fact, in the presence of HK firms may even invest to find which are more profitable to able to reduce their every employee's abnormal working hours daily rather than normal number of working hours of their every employee.

Bibliography
Economic And Trade Information On Hong Kong, (14 Aug. 2012). Hong Kong Government Forecast for 2012, retrieved from the following URL: http://www.cepa.hktdc.com
Middison A. (2001). The World Economy. A Millennial Perspective, OECD, Paris.
Yasuhio, U. (2014). Japan Labor Review, vol.11 no.3,
High Economic Growth And Human Capital:
Conditions For Sustained Growth, Konan
University.
William, C&Wing, S.(1997). The Hong Kong Economic
Policy Studies Series, published by City University
Of HK Press, Hong Kong